insight text guide

Melanie Napthine

Ghost Wall

Sarah Moss

First published in 2024.

Insight Publications Pty Ltd
3/350 Charman Road
Cheltenham VIC 3192
Australia
Tel: +61 3 8571 4950
Email: books@insightpublications.com.au

www.insightpublications.com.au

Sarah Moss' *Ghost Wall* / Melanie Napthine

Melanie Napthine asserts the moral right to be identified as the author of this work.

ISBNs:
9781923154872 (print)
9781923154865 (digital)

Cover design and layout by Melisa Paredes
Edited by Julia Carlomagno
Proofread by Penny Mansley

Printed by Markono Print Media Pte Ltd

contents

CHARACTER MAP

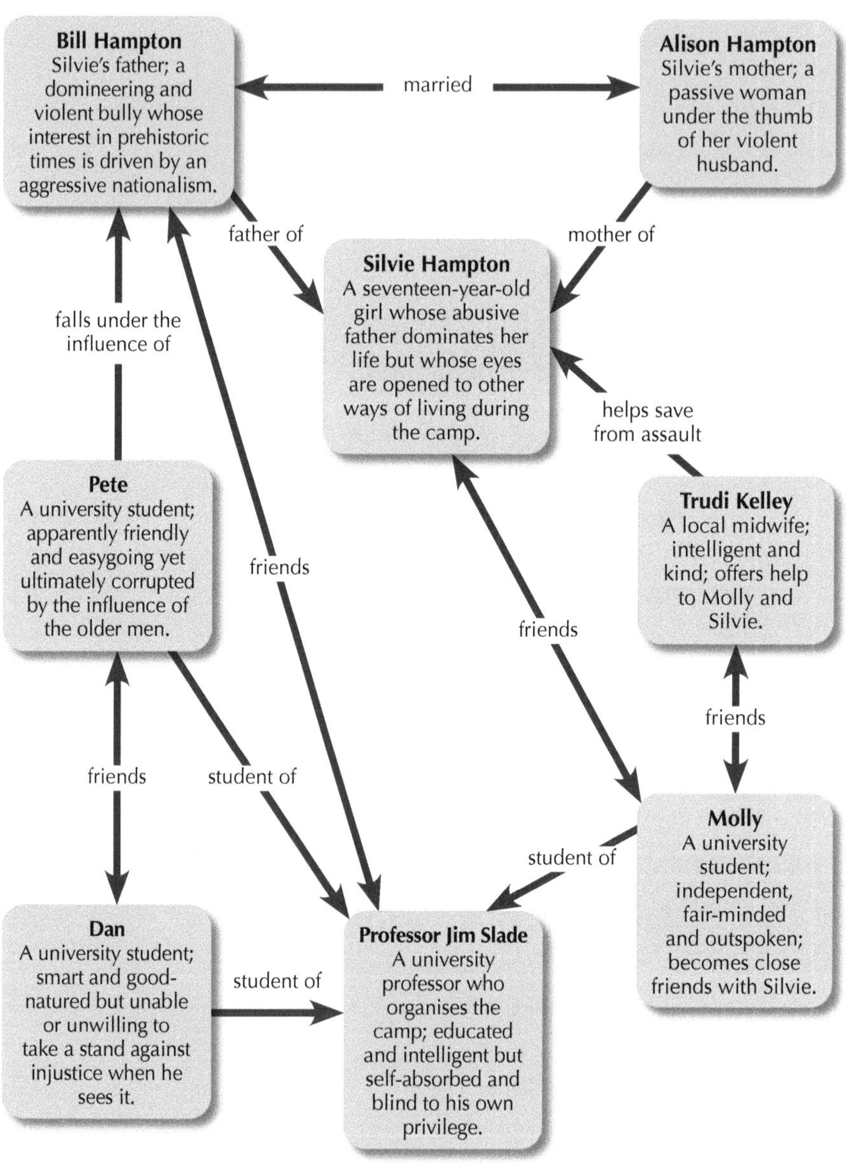

OVERVIEW

About the author

Born in Glasgow, Scotland, in 1975, Sarah Moss moved with her family to Manchester, in the north of England, at the age of two. Moss' mother worked in the arts and in healthcare, while her father was a computer scientist. As a child, Moss spent a lot of time outside, particularly on family holidays to the Peak District, an area of the Pennine Hills dominated by the Peak District National Park. As an adult, she continues to enjoy the outdoor pursuit of running, which appeals to her because it is 'about being out in a body, feet on the stones and rain in the hair' (Brockes 2021). This interest in the physical body and its resilience and limitations is evident in *Ghost Wall*, as well as in much of Moss' other work. So, too, is her interest in weather, especially bad weather. She has observed:

> I think the reason I'm interested in 'bad' weather is because that is when you're most aware of your own embodiment in the world … You really know you're alive when you're most physically present to the world and the elements. (Brockes 2021)

After graduating from secondary school, she attended the University of Oxford, where she earned a Bachelor of Arts, a Master of Studies and a Doctor of Philosophy (PhD) in English Literature. She took up a lecturing position at the University of Kent in 2004 and remained there until 2009, the year that her first novel, *Cold Earth*, was published.

Following this, Moss moved with her family to Iceland, where she taught at the University of Iceland. Her memoir of this year abroad, *Names for the Sea: Strangers in Iceland*, was shortlisted for the Royal Society of Literature's Ondaatje Prize in 2013.

Returning to England from Iceland, Moss was appointed Senior Lecturer in Literature and Place at Exeter University's Penryn Campus in Cornwall. She later took up a position as Director of the Warwick Writing Programme at the University of Warwick, teaching creative writing.

Moss has received a number of accolades for her writing. In addition to the Ondaatje Prize shortlisting for her Icelandic memoir, her 2011 novel *Night Waking* was selected for the Jerwood Fiction Uncovered Prize in 2011, and her novels *Bodies of Light, Signs for Lost Children* and *The Tidal Zone* were shortlisted for the Wellcome Book Prize in 2015, 2016 and 2017 respectively. She has also written a number of academic works.

Ghost Wall was published in 2018 to a critically favourable reception: the novel was shortlisted for both the Ondaatje Prize and the Polari Prize, and longlisted for the 2019 Women's Prize for Fiction.

Moss is married and has two sons.

Synopsis

Sulevia Hampton (known as Silvie) and her parents Bill and Alison join a summer camp organised by Professor Jim Slade for three of his senior archaeology students. Silvie's father has paid for his family to take part in the camp after having connected with the Professor due to their shared interest in British history – in particular, the Iron Age period. The group establishes a campsite in a rural area where they intend to try to live as Iron Age Britons did, hunting and gathering their own foods and avoiding contact with the modern world.

Their dedication to this project varies. Bus driver Bill, for whom history is a passion, is committed to authenticity as far as practicably possible, forcing his wife and daughter to wear rough tunics as their forebears would have, and insisting they sleep together in the roundhouse, built by the students 'as part of a course on "experiential archaeology"' (p.6). He would prefer that the entire group stay together in this structure, 'if the students wanted a real experience' (p.7). Professor Slade is more pragmatic, recognising that 'after all authenticity was impossible' and that the 'flavour of Iron Age life' (p.7) was a more reasonable goal; he and the students therefore sleep in their own tents.

This difference in approach to the camp causes some tension, as does Bill's belligerent attitude, particularly towards the women in the group. Accustomed to issuing commands to his wife and daughter, he also tries to take charge at the camp but meets with resistance from the independent and self-assured Molly. Though she joins in with the other students and Silvie to forage for food while the Professor and Bill hunt for game and fish, she is also happy to break the rules of the camp – for instance, by visiting the local convenience store for food items considered contraband within the camp. She encourages Silvie to join her in such illicit activities and Silvie does so, though reluctantly, in constant fear of being found out and punished by her father.

Although she envies the students' freedom and ease in the world, Silvie soon proves herself more knowledgeable and capable when it comes to survival and practical skills. Despite this, Silvie and the students' attempts at gathering sufficient natural produce to feed the group do not always go particularly well, and Bill chastises them for their lack of success. Bill also disagrees with the Professor about Iron Age contact between the Romans and the people then inhabiting what is now Britain: Bill views these early Britons as strong warriors and defenders of their land, and also as somehow quintessentially British in a way he contrasts favourably with the more diverse Britain of the current day. The Professor, however, points out that these early Britons would not have recognised themselves as an entity in that way.

Due to Bill's strident opinions and domineering nature, Molly quickly identifies him as a bully. She is horrified to learn that he uses physical violence to control both Alison and Silvie when she sees the marks left on Silvie's back and legs after Bill beats her with a belt for bathing topless in a stream. Molly tells Silvie, 'it's not OK for someone to hit you' (p.126), a clear and simple statement of her right to bodily autonomy and safety that Silvie, at this point, is not ready to truly believe.

Following one hunting trip, Bill and the Professor return 'het up' (p.102) with the thrill of a new idea. With the help of the male students, they set about constructing a 'ghost wall' – a wall of skulls such as the Iron Age peoples of the area would have constructed to intimidate their enemies. The Iron Age peoples used human skulls; however, their modern-day imitators must make do with animal skulls, including those of the rabbits they killed and ate, as well as cow and sheep skulls purchased by the Professor from the market in town. That evening, the group – with the exception of Alison, who stays in the tent, and Molly, who decides to go into town – gather around the wall to drum and chant until the early hours. Silvie is equally caught up in the excitement without quite understanding why.

The next day, the Professor takes Silvie aside to propose an idea: they would like her to play the role of sacrificial victim in a re-enactment of a ritual murder of the sort believed to have caused the deaths of the bog people found in the area. Though she is frightened at the prospect, under considerable pressure from her father, she agrees, feeling she has no choice.

The men assure Silvie she will not be harmed in the re-enactment, and she is bound and taken to the nearby bog. There, she is stripped and beaten with sticks and stones by the men, who have become intoxicated by the atmosphere, their power and a kind of mass hysteria that causes them to lose all control, with the possible exception of Dan, who leaves 'quite early' (p.146).

Ultimately, Silvie is saved from sharing the fate of the bog-girl her father told her about – whose sacrifice at the hands of her friends and family opens the novel – when the police arrive to free her. Molly, outraged at the men's 'insane' (p.139) proposal to torment Silvie in this way, had sought out Trudi, the midwife she and Silvie had met on an earlier trip to the convenience store, and together they had called the police. The novel ends with Silvie and Molly spending the night at Trudi's house, safe in the knowledge that Bill, having been taken into custody, can do them no further harm.

Character summaries

Silvie (Sulevia) Hampton

Seventeen-year-old Silvie is the protagonist and narrator of *Ghost Wall*. She is the only child of Bill and Alison, and a reluctant participant in the camp on which the novel centres. Silvie has been trained to submit to the will of her aggressive father, to the point that she finds it difficult to identify, much less to follow, her own inclinations and beliefs.

Bill Hampton

The interests and beliefs of Silvie's father, Bill, shape the lives of his immediate family, including during the time at their rural camp. He tolerates no dissent when it comes to his strongly held opinions, and uses violence against both his wife and his child to ensure their obedience to him. His domineering attitude causes friction in the camp, with Molly in particular resenting and resisting his attempts to assert complete control over proceedings.

Alison Hampton

Silvie's mother, Alison, occupies a traditional domestic role both within her family and at the camp, where she is responsible for preparing meals and keeping the site clean. Alison is obedient to and fearful of her domineering and abusive husband, Bill. This controlling relationship has led to her suppressing her own desires and beliefs.

Professor Jim Slade

Professor Slade is the organiser and official leader of the camp, although he takes a more relaxed approach to the quest for historical authenticity than Bill, and his students tend to take their cues from him. He is intelligent and educated, and begins by taking on the role of leader of the camp. He also displays some skill when it comes to hunting. However, his interpersonal skills are less developed, as shown by his apparent obliviousness to the abuse Silvie and Alison are suffering.

Molly

One of the university students taking part in the camp, Molly becomes close to Silvie over the course of the novel, despite sometimes struggling to understand her circumstances and attitude towards her father. Molly is outspoken and unafraid to defy authority – in particular, Bill – when she feels it necessary, a habit that causes Silvie considerable anxiety.

Dan

Dan is another of Professor Slade's archaeology students who joins the camp. He is friendly and interested in Silvie's life and circumstances, which are very different from his own. He displays some misogyny in his jokes about women, but he also evinces some vulnerability – for instance, when he vomits upon witnessing the skinning of the rabbits. When the sacrificial ritual begins he takes part only reluctantly, and shows concern for Silvie's welfare. Ultimately, he leaves before she is injured, though he does nothing to help her.

Pete

Pete is the third university student on the camp. Like Dan, he is initially friendly towards Silvie and good-humoured in the face of the privations of camp life. But he is easily caught up in the fervour that causes the men to take the ritual re-enactment too far, to the point of causing physical injury to Silvie. He thus exemplifies the consequences of mass hysteria and the ease with which a veneer of respectability and civilisation can be removed to expose an animalistic or primitive nature.

Trudi Kelley

Midwife Trudi lives in the village nearest to where the group is camped. She meets Silvie and Molly at the Spar convenience store and expresses interest in their summer project. Later, it is Trudi to whom Molly turns for help when Silvie is forced to take part in the sacrificial ritual, and Trudi's house in which the girls finally take refuge.

Louise

Louise is the basket-weaver who visits the camp, at the Professor's request, to teach the campers about basket-weaving. Cheerful, thoughtful and empathetic, Louise is able, through her work, to bring to life the past and to imagine the lives of those long gone. Though she is a minor character, her visit is the catalyst for Silvie to reflect more deeply on the nature and purpose of their camp project, and also on the complexities of her father's own fascination with the past.

BACKGROUND & CONTEXT

Ghost Wall was longlisted for the Women's Prize for Fiction, one of the United Kingdom's most prestigious literary awards, in 2019. In an interview about the honour, Moss describes her inspiration for the novel as stemming from time spent at a writing residency for the Hexham Book Festival. Hexham, in the north of England, lies close to Hadrian's Wall, a defensive structure that spans England from west to east. The wall was begun in 122 AD, when Britain, then known as Britannia, was under the rule of Roman Emperor Hadrian. Moss recounts becoming fascinated with the wall, which she describes as having been intended as a 'boundary between the Roman empire and the barbarians' (Women's Prize for Fiction 2019). She began reflecting on borders more generally, such as those 'between civilisation and barbarity, nature and culture, insiders and outsiders' (Women's Prize for Fiction 2019). This interest in boundaries, and their permeability, is a theme of *Ghost Wall* – the campers, to varying degrees, pit themselves against the modern world, and the borders between the past and the present, and even between life and death, are shown to be porous.

The Iron Age

Moss has said that she 'read everything [she] could find' about Iron Age Britain in preparation for writing *Ghost Wall* (Women's Prize for Fiction 2019). The Iron Age in Britain, beginning around 800 BC, earned its name because it was the period during which ironworking techniques and processes were brought to Britain from continental Europe. The age is considered to have ended in 43 AD following the Roman invasion of Britain, though its ending was neither absolute nor abrupt.

Iron Age Britain was primarily agricultural. As Professor Slade in *Ghost Wall* notes, the people of this period would not have considered themselves British, or as belonging to a single nation. Rather, they were a collection of Celtic tribes ruled by chieftains or kings. Within their communities, they were organised into extended family units, or clans. The most popular style of dwelling was the roundhouse, like the one the students build in *Ghost Wall*, with a hearth or fire in the centre of the room, like the one Alison cooks over.

Religious festivals and customs were important to Iron Age communities. Two such important occasions were Beltane in March, which celebrated the beginning of summer, and Samhain in November, which marked the harvest period and the end of the warm season. Sacrifices – material, animal and human – were a significant aspect of these sorts of religious events. At least some of the bog people referred to in *Ghost Wall* are thought by historians to have been victims of such sacrifices.

Bog bodies have been discovered in many places in Europe, including Denmark, Germany, Estonia and the United Kingdom. The fascination they hold for contemporary people lies at least in part in their unusually preserved state, a result of the unique physical conditions of bogs. Bog people have been discovered with their clothes intact, and even their facial expressions preserved. The marks of their unusual deaths, such as ropes around their necks and stab wounds, are also evident in some bog people. While it cannot be known exactly why these individuals were selected for sacrifice, historian Melanie Giles has noted the importance of bogs to Iron Age communities, describing them as 'liminal spaces' due to being both land and water, yet not entirely either element, and as 'deep ... thin places ... where the sacred might be touched and the supernatural made manifest' (Hilts 2021).

This interest in 'in-between' places and states is shared by Moss, who describes how the bog-girl whose death opens the novel is held by her tormentors 'in the time and space between life and death' (p.3). Moss has spoken of her interest in fascination with boundaries. →

> I'm interested in boundaries of all kinds, including the ones we set ourselves and rely on other people to set themselves. One of the horrors of the last few years has been watching the fracture of consensus about what should not be expressed, and I wanted to explore how we give ourselves and each other incremental permission to do harm. (Women's Prize for Fiction 2019)

The novel takes its title from a custom associated with Iron Age Britons – the construction of a 'ghost wall', or wall made out of human skulls, intended to frighten enemy combatants. There is some debate among historians as to whether such walls, at least in the sense that they are described in *Ghost Wall*, actually existed.

Modern-day Britain

In 2016, a referendum was held in the UK in which citizens were asked to vote on whether the country should remain a part of the European Union (EU) of nations. Those who wanted the country to leave the EU were victorious, by a narrow margin, and the UK officially left the EU in January 2020, in a move commonly referred to as 'Brexit' (a portmanteau of the words 'Britain' and 'exit'). While stopping short of citing this significant political change as inspiration for or an explicit concern of *Ghost Wall*, Moss acknowledges that 'it would be hard for a writer to live in the UK and not write about Brexit in some way. It's haunted the terrors and dreams and plans and conversations of everyone I know for nearly three years' (Women's Prize for Fiction 2019).

Brexit exposed a deep division within the UK between those who became known as 'remainers' (who wanted the UK to remain part of the EU) and 'leavers' (those who voted for the UK to leave the EU). While motivations for voting in either direction were varied and complex, the popular characterisation of 'leavers' depicts them as politically conservative, nostalgic for a mythical time in which a 'purer' British culture existed, and even racist. In *Ghost Wall*, Bill could be understood to represent the sort of thinking associated with supporters of Brexit, with his suspicion and dislike of 'Negroes' (p.24) and 'Pakis' (p.25), and his preoccupation with the notion that in Iron Age times, Britons – despite not being known by that name or even recognising themselves as a unified group – were brave, resourceful and powerful, qualities apparently eroded and undermined by modern ways of living and a more pluralistic society.

Class

The north of England is a frequent setting in Moss' work, and class differences, often represented by the north–south divide in England, is a theme to which she returns. She has spoken and written frequently about her northern upbringing and the ways in which this has shaped her. In an article about treating herself to a piece of jewellery in Paris, she reflects that she continues to hear her 'ancestors howling in [her] ears' (Moss 2022), dissuading her from spending too much money on frivolous or unnecessary things. She describes a patisserie as 'too grand, not for the likes of me', a sentiment that echoes the way Silvie in *Ghost Wall* feels about many of the students' privileges.

Moss has also spoken about 'sunken class biases and assumptions' (Brockes 2021) in relation to Covid lockdowns in the UK. She decried the ways in which these impacted far more negatively on the less privileged, including those whose homes were not sanctuaries or safe places, 'a huge number of people, mostly women and children' (Moss in Clark 2021), like Silvie and her mother. Though *Ghost Wall* was written prior to the pandemic, it evinces Moss' concern for those with limited access to power. Similarly, she has described family holidays as a 'kind of lockdown' (Moss 2020), and the claustrophobic atmosphere, deprivation and simmering tensions in *Ghost Wall* support this analogy.

Women's rights

Writing in a post-MeToo world, Moss is able to assume in her readers a certain level of awareness of the dangers of coercive control. Even before his capacity for physical violence is revealed, Bill's controlling behaviour is apparent in his insistence on the group sitting around the fire on his first night, and on Silvie sleeping with her parents in the roundhouse – though she would rather be in a tent like the students – so that he can keep a careful eye on her. This is largely with the aim of restricting or suppressing her sexuality – 'of course you can't sleep wi' the lads, shame on you' (p.7) – though Silvie exhibits no sexual interest in the 'lads' and is in fact far more fascinated by Molly's bared body.

Molly's ease in her own physicality and conviction in her own opinions, particularly when it comes to feminist issues, reflect contemporary mores (customs). In modern Britain – and Australia – there is broad agreement that men and women are equal, and that attempts by men to restrict women's autonomy are unacceptable. Bill, on the other hand, does not accept this notion, as evidenced by his brutality towards the women in his family, and his fierce disapproval of Molly, which is not just a result of her outspokenness, but also of her sexual openness. Bill would seem to subscribe to the 'Madonna–whore' dichotomy, an attitude towards women that involves separating them into two distinct groups. The first consists of those who are 'good' wives and mothers, in the image of Jesus' mother Mary, obedient and without sexual desires. The other group are considered 'bad' or corrupt due to a willingness to indulge their own sexual urges. Bill accuses his daughter of behaving like a 'whore' (p.62) when she bathes without her top on. In this he reflects an attitude that belongs to a much earlier time, when women were generally viewed as inferior to men and punished for behaving in ways associated with masculinity, such as sexual frankness.

But Bill is also representative of a type of contemporary masculinity promulgated by conservative thinkers such as Jordan Peterson and Andrew Tate, who promote the idea that there are essential and important differences between men and women and that denying or transgressing these boundaries is harmful on both an individual and a societal level. At its most extreme, this school of thought advocates for men to exercise control over women even to the point of physical violence, just as Bill does over his wife and child.

GENRE, STRUCTURE & LANGUAGE

Genre

Ghost Wall draws on, and might be categorised as belonging to, multiple genres. In literature, the pastoral tradition is considered to have begun in the classical period with a series of poems known as bucolics by the Greek poet Theocritus (who was born in approximately 300 BC and died in or after 260 BC). In England, the pastoral became popularised first in the sixteenth century through the work of such writers as Edmund Spenser, and again in the eighteenth century in the work of poets such as Andrew Marvell. The pastoral tradition glorifies nature and the lives of those who exist closely with it, such as shepherds. In pastoral poetry, plays and novels, idyllic rural life is contrasted with the corruption of urban existence. *Ghost Wall*'s Bill exemplifies this attitude in his desire to return to nature and to what he views as a simpler, purer way of living.

Ghost Wall alludes to the pastoral, with its rural setting and the characters' attempts to re-create a time during which people – at least those of a certain class and circumstance – had to live and work closely with nature, gathering their own foods and fashioning tools by hand. But it quickly undermines the notion that such an existence is morally superior to or more desirable than urban life, with its conveniences and complexities. The campers struggle to nourish themselves adequately with what they can find on the land, and the reader is reminded that life in the actual Iron Age was often short, difficult and brutal.

Ghost Wall might also be considered a bildungsroman, or coming-of-age story, in which the protagonist moves from childhood to adulthood, trading their innocence for experience. The seeds of this transition for Silvie are evident from the start of the novel, in her scepticism about her father's mission on the camp. By the end of the novel, she has presumably properly escaped his control over her life, as he is arrested for his abuse of her during the sacrificial ritual. *Ghost Wall* also alludes to Silvie's sexual awakening, as she displays an increasing interest in and affection for Molly, not only as an example of the kind of young woman she herself might be if it weren't for her controlling father, but also for her physical form. The closing scene of the novel dwells on the entwined bodies of the pair as Silvie seeks comfort in Molly's 'bare legs cradling mine, her fingers at rest on my belly' (p.149).

The novel also draws on features and tropes of the Gothic horror and suspense genres. Although *Ghost Wall* is largely set outdoors, the group's isolation and dependence on one another create a claustrophobic atmosphere in which interpersonal conflicts constantly threaten to spill over into violence. The extended episode involving the skinning and preparing of the slaughtered rabbits is visceral and disturbing, the rabbits an analogy for innocence destroyed.

Ghost Wall is also in some ways a survivalist text. The survivalism genre depicts human beings as at the mercy of the implacable forces of nature, such as the weather and predatory animals. In this genre, protagonists must develop resilience, physical and mental strength, and a healthy respect for nature's power in order to survive. Well-known examples of survivalist fiction include Daniel Defoe's *Robinson Crusoe*, William Golding's *Lord of the Flies* and Gary Paulsen's *Hatchet*. By situating themselves in a rural setting and denying themselves modern conveniences and tools, the campers in *Ghost Wall* are challenged to survive with only their wits and physical resilience. The twist, however, is that for Silvie, the gravest danger she must confront is not the environment but her own abusive father.

Structure

The novel is not divided into chapters or sections but rather takes its shape from the passing days. There is a sameness to the routine quickly established at camp, with Bill and the Professor spending their time hunting, Silvie and the students foraging for edible plants and Alison cooking and tending the camp. This is reflected in the novel's structure, which follows the daily rhythms of waking, 'finding and gathering, walking and squatting, talking and scattering' (p.106), and sleeping.

The events that relieve this pattern are quotidian (ordinary) – the slaughter and dressing of the rabbits, the clandestine visits to the convenience store, Silvie's naked bathing (for which she is harshly punished). Yet it is through such relatively mundane occurrences that tension is built. An atmosphere of fear grows to permeate the group, and the friction between its members – particularly between Bill and Molly – increasingly threatens to spill over into violence.

The novel also adopts a circular structure, opening with a description of an unnamed young woman being led to her slow death at the edge of a bog (the 'water-earth', p.3) by her fellow community members, who strip her, shave her head and tie a rope around her neck while 'her neighbours and her family' (p.2) watch silently on. Later, the reader will learn of the bog people with whom both Bill and Silvie are fascinated – individuals whose bodies, naturally mummified by the acidic water, low temperatures and lack of oxygen in peat bogs, have been discovered in various boggy locations around the world. Experts have conjectured that some of these individuals, particularly those found in Britain, might have been tortured and sacrificed by their community for religious or other, unknown, reasons.

There are clear parallels between the girl in the novel's opening – later suggested to be the bog girl whose photo Bill shows his daughter – and Silvie, who experiences similar treatment at the novel's end, in a ritual intended to mimic those practised by earlier Britons.

Language

The novel is narrated in the first person by Silvie and the tone reflects her character: at once pragmatic and colloquial ('I'd bugger off now if I was you, mate', she imagines a raven calling to her and the students, p.20), and capable of fine observation and lyricism. She often narrates as she thinks, in fragments and meandering sentences – for example, when she decides how to spend one early morning.

> No wind, the dawn still … Up onto the moor, I thought, sunrise, why not, although I knew that there's nowhere to hide up there, that if he [her father] woke and came that way, after more rabbits perhaps, he would see me anywhere within a five-mile radius, even if that also meant he would see that I was alone and not consorting with men. (p.72)

Silvie and her family also use the dialect of their Northern English home. For example, Silvie refers to a 'ginnel' (a northern term for an alleyway) and she and her parents frequently use the word 'summat' (meaning 'something'). The differences in language and accent between Silvie's family and the others from the university in the south of England reflect more than just regional variation. They also represent class differences, which become a source of tension within the group, the south of England being often associated with relative social and economic privilege compared to the less advantaged north.

Terminology drawn from nature, including the names of a wide variety of plants, is another notable language feature. Moss' detailed descriptions of the land are intimate and visceral, depicting both its beauty and its harshness. The bogs are a key example: important and even sacred places to Iron Age Britons, in which the treasures of generations are preserved, they are also sites of torture and murder. Silvie recalls her own fall into the bog in language that is both intimate and haunting.

> The bog seals around you, and it will of course go further than skin, or at least will fill the inner skins of every orifice, rising like a tide in your lungs, creeping cold into your vagina, it will embalm you from the inside out. (p.98)

Symbolism

Symbolism is also a feature of *Ghost Wall*. One prominent example is the rabbits, whose death and dismemberment represent innocence destroyed, paralleling, troublingly, Silvie's treatment at the hands of her father.

Another instance is the ghost wall itself, which signifies the blurred boundaries between the living and the dead, decorated as it is with skulls that retain the power to induce fear and affect the behaviour of those who behold them. The wall is also reflective of the primitivism or baser urges that transcend time because they are innately human.

DAY-BY-DAY ANALYSIS

Prologue (pp.1–3)

Summary: *At dusk, a nameless woman or girl (her age is unspecified at this point) is led by a group of people referred to only as 'they' (p.1) to the edge of what the reader later understands to be a bog. Here, before an audience of neighbours, friends and family members, she is stripped of her loose tunic and her head is shaved until she 'doesn't look like one of them' (p.2). A rope is placed around her neck and the collection of weapons nearby – 'the sharpened willow withies, the pile of stones, the small blades' (p.3) – hint at the intentions of the group. This is made explicit in the final sentence of the prologue, which explains that she will eventually, though not soon, 'be quite dead' (p.3).*

The eerie and portentous opening to *Ghost Wall* leaves the reader troubled and disoriented. Little context is given for the scene described, no participants are named, no time period is specified, and the immediate violation of, and imminent violence towards, the 'she' depicted is shocking. Equally shocking is the apparent collusion of the crowd that watches, which includes her sisters and brother, children she had played with, 'people who held her hands as she learnt to walk' (p.2). The fact that she had been 'one of them, ordinary' (p.2) and yet now faces death at their hands for no apparent reason leaves the reader wondering at the motivations of the woman's captors and the witnesses to her murder.

The victim herself, however, is apparently resigned to her gruesome fate. Though she 'shakes' in 'fear' (p.1) and even 'keen[s]' (p.2) in sorrow or panic, she does not actively resist what is being done to her. Given that 'everyone knows what is coming' (p.1) and that 'there are no surprises' (p.2), it is clear that this is some sort of ritual important to this community, though its origins and aims are, at this point, obscure to the reader.

Key point

Though chronologically and in terms of plot the prologue is disconnected from the other events in *Ghost Wall*, it immediately establishes the atmosphere of tension and violence that will increasingly pervade the novel. It also encapsulates many of the novel's key preoccupations, including the human capacity for cruelty, liminal states such as that between life and death, a focus on the strengths and vulnerabilities of the body, and the power of the group.

Key vocabulary

Withies: strong, flexible willow branches.

Q Why do you think it might be important to the community that the sacrificial victim is both one of them and yet made to appear unlike them before her death?

Day One (pp.4–9)

Summary: *On their first evening at the camp in rural Northern England, Silvie, her parents, Professor Slade and the three university students gather around a fire, at Bill's insistence, waiting for darkness to descend before retiring to bed. Silvie and her mother have trouble sleeping but Bill apparently sleeps deeply, snoring like 'a serrated knife through cardboard' (p.9).*

The novel opens with the group of seven – Silvie's family and the university group – gathered around a fire built by Bill. Though the rest of the group are 'bored', Bill's 'force of will' (p.5) keeps them there, an early indication of his dominating personality. His wife sits where he has instructed her to, and when Silvie leaves the circle to relieve herself, Bill is quick to manage even that personal process, ordering her to move far away from the campsite lest the young men see her.

Silvie and her parents, again at Bill's insistence, will sleep in the roundhouse constructed by the students during a course on 'experiential archaeology' (p.6). Bill would have preferred that the entire group occupy this dwelling, as he believes Iron Age Britons would have cohabited, but the students insist on sleeping in their own tents. Silvie, too, would prefer the privacy of her own tent but her father will not allow it. As she often does, Silvie allows herself mutinous thoughts she mostly does not dare to speak, reflecting that:

> I do not know what my father thought I might want to do in those days but he devoted considerable attention to making sure I couldn't do it. (p.8)

It is thus clear that Silvie resents the control her father exerts over her but feels unable to express this, at least not directly. When she complains of his snoring to her mother that night, Alison is quick to hush her daughter and the pair of them lie 'frozen' (p.9), presumably in fear, when the snoring abruptly but momentarily stops. When Silvie wonders, during this lull, if her father will breathe again or if this is 'the end' (p.9), the startling notion confirms to the reader that relations within the small family are clearly not harmonious, whatever front they may present to the wider world.

Key vocabulary

Summat: Northern English slang for 'something'.

Q What do you think Silvie's father is anxious about Silvie doing if he doesn't maintain constant supervision of her?

Q What do the students' 'inauthentic and colourful waterproof nylon tents' (p.7) suggest about their attitude towards the camp?

Day Two (pp.9–46)

Summary: *Silvie and the students are sent out to gather food while Bill and the Professor go fishing and Alison stays at the camp to prepare food and tidy up. Silvie takes the lead on their expedition, surprising the students with her knowledge of the natural world when she guides them to find bilberries in the heather, as well as thyme to season fish or* *griddle cakes (batter cooked on a griddle). In the afternoon, the group is visited by Louise, who runs a class on basket-weaving for the students, which Silvie joins. Silvie reflects on previous trips taken with her father, to a museum and to walk the length of Hadrian's Wall. That evening, Bill and the Professor debate their different understandings of the interactions between Romans and the inhabitants of Britain at the time the wall was built.*

The Professor takes charge on the second day, doling out tasks to the others. Bill tells Silvie to join the students foraging, which she is happy enough to do. As she and the students get to know each other, the differences between them quickly become apparent. Molly has never heard of some of the major northern towns near where Silvie lives, and she is puzzled by Bill's interest in history, given his profession as a bus driver. Dan's casual assumption that Silvie must be planning to study archaeology at university makes Silvie uncomfortable – 'stop questioning me, I thought' (p.21) – because it highlights the extent to which her own upbringing and education have failed to provide her with such options.

The students are impressed, however, with her knowledge of plants, which she attributes to her father's teaching. She steers them towards a place to forage for bilberries, passing the road to Hadrian's Wall, which she and her father had hiked the length of the previous year. Her recollection of the trip exposes many of Bill's qualities that will later cause friction in the camp, particularly his nostalgia for a Britain that he feels no longer exists. On their visit to the rundown docks near the wall, his tone is both sorrowful and disgusted when he tells Silvie, 'Used to send ships all over the world from here. Look at it now' (p.25). His references to 'Negroes' (p.24) and 'Paki' (p.25) food clearly demonstrate the link he draws between multiculturalism and the loss of an 'original Britishness' (p.20).

There is another aspect to Bill's interest in history, however. 'He likes dead things' (p.40), Silvie tells Molly, a fact illuminated by her recollection of another trip she took with her father, to a museum to view the preserved remains of a bog person. His fascination with the more brutal aspects of prehistoric culture is evident when he tells Silvie how the man died, 'pushed in … and a rope around his neck and all' (p.39).

The Professor and the students, meanwhile, do not view history or the camp's intent in the same light. The debate between Bill and the Professor that evening about Britons' resistance to the Romans demonstrates this divide. The Professor has gained his knowledge systematically, through the formal education system; he is interested in facts and evidence and is quick to correct Bill's mispronunciations. Bill, on the other hand, is self-taught, and his interpretation of people and events is significantly shaped by his passions and prejudices. When the Professor reminds him that early Britons were mostly Celts, Bill 'didn't like this line' (p.45), complicating as it does his romantic view of prehistoric Britain as a noble and united nation.

Key point

Though Silvie is steered by her father's will and, as a child, has little choice but to accompany him on his trips, she does demonstrate an independent and genuine interest in both history and nature, as shown by her engagement with Louise's basket-weaving and her recognition of the connection between the past and the present: 'we ourselves became the ghosts' (p.34).

Key vocabulary

Bannock: a type of flatbread usually made with oats or barley.

Boudicca: a famous queen of the Celtic Iceni tribe, who led a revolt against the Romans.

Byre: a cowshed.

Calyx: the outer part of a flower.

Carnyces: trumpet-like instruments used in battle by Iron Age Celts.

CND badge: a badge in support of the Campaign for Nuclear Disarmament.

Damson: a plum-like fruit.

Ergot: a fungus that grows on rye and other cereals; ingestion can cause serious illness.

Lummock: a slang word for a stupid or lazy person.

Mort: a lot; many.

OS map: an Ordnance Survey map; a detailed map of an area, popular in Britain.

Paki: an offensive term for a person of Pakistani origin.

Spar: one of a chain of popular convenience stores.

Stile: a wooden structure that allows people (but not animals) to climb over a fence between fields.

Trivet: a metal stand to support cooking vessels.

Winsome: charming.

Q What is the significance of Silvie's favourite possession being a toy owl?

Day Three (pp.46–71)

Summary: *Bill and the Professor set traps to catch rabbits. Silvie and the students go to the beach to forage. The students strip down to their underwear to swim but Silvie ventures only thigh-deep, keeping her tunic on. Back at the camp, Silvie bathes in a muddy pool to wash the sand off herself and soothe her sunburn. Shortly after she removes her top, as Molly had done at the beach, she is surprised by her father and the Professor, returning with captured rabbits. Bill beats Silvie with a belt for exposing herself. After lunch, the group skin the rabbits. In bed that night, unable to sleep, Silvie recalls the bog-girl her father had once showed her a picture of, who had been tortured and killed by her community.*

The trip to the beach is a pivotal experience for Silvie. Already intrigued and unsettled by the students' confidence, she is deeply fascinated by the ease with which they discuss anatomy and strip down to their underwear to bathe. She finds herself attracted to Molly, whom she 'suddenly wanted to touch' (p.56). This attraction is physical, as evidenced by the way in which Silvie lingers on the details of Molly's body, her 'outdoor colour' (p.56), the 'water beading on the curve of [her] shoulders' (p.57). But it is also emotional: she is as fascinated by Molly's confidence as by her physicality. Just as she follows in Molly's footsteps on their way home, she mimics her when she herself removes her clothing to bathe in the stream back at camp.

The beating Silvie receives from Bill for doing so demonstrates the connection between his need to dominate and his deep misogyny. He is fearful of and disgusted by the notion of his daughter as a sexual being, a 'little whore' (p.62), not merely out of a misguided desire to protect her but also because it is a reminder that she is an individual with her own wants and desires, not merely a possession of his.

Bill's brutality with the dead rabbits, and his hostility towards Molly regarding her reluctance to take part in the skinning, might be understood as stemming in part from displaced anger towards his daughter. His rage has not quite been satiated by the beating, and he takes a sadistic pleasure in describing how to skin and cut up the rabbits. There are clear parallels between the dead creatures and Silvie and her mother, all innocent and unwitting victims of Bill's (and the Professor's) violence. Moreover, the fact that Silvie repeatedly wonders how exactly the rabbits were killed echoes the mystery of the deaths of the bog people, who 'rarely had only one way to die' (p.70), like the young woman on whom Silvie dwells as she struggles to sleep due to the pain of the beating.

Key vocabulary

Flint knapping: shaping tools out of stone.

Impalpable: unable to be felt or understood.

Mithering: Northern English slang for complaining.

Samphire: an edible plant that grows near the sea.

Q Why do you think Bill apologises to the Professor when they see Silvie bathing in the pool?

Q Bill's reaction to Silvie bathing seems to support Molly's statement about 'men's fear of women's bodies' (p.55). What other examples of this fear can you identify in the text?

Day Four (pp.71–104)

Summary: *While they are both toileting in the woods, Molly sees the wounds inflicted on Silvie by Bill. Bill orders Silvie to joint the rabbits, but Dan volunteers himself and Pete to do it so that Molly and Silvie can escape the camp for a while. They make an illicit visit to the Spar, where they meet local midwife Trudi, who takes an interest in their camping experiment and invites them to visit her anytime. The men return late to camp after Pete falls into a bog. The two older men are excited about an idea they do not share with the others. The group have a conversation about bog sacrifices and their own dearest possessions.*

When Molly notices the belt marks on Silvie's back, she is concerned, but Silvie immediately explains them away as 'sunburn' (p.74), suggesting that she is accustomed to covering up her father's abuse. She has also been trained in endurance, reflecting that 'she could and would' get through the day despite the extreme pain she is suffering, since 'it was not as if there was an alternative' (p.75). However, she also demonstrates that her spirit has not been entirely crushed. She is able, for instance, to answer her father back, 'want[ing] him to know I still had a mind and a voice' (p.76), and she finds some relief in escaping his oversight when she leaves the camp with Molly, thinking of it as like 'sneaking out of school at break to buy sweets' (p.77).

Molly encourages Silvie to defy her father further by visiting the Spar for snacks. Here they meet Trudi Kelley, a friendly local midwife who invites them to come to her if ever they need advice or a hot shower. Her gentle ridicule of men – 'poor dears' (p.84) – contrasts starkly with Silvie's fear of her father, whose surveillance of her has trained her to feel that somehow 'he'll know' (p.85) about their contraband from the Spar. Molly tells her, 'you're terrified of him' (p.85) but Silvie denies it. Though she and Molly are growing closer and she appreciates Molly's tenderness towards her, such as when Molly takes her hand after she stumbles, she is not yet ready to overturn a lifelong habit of loyalty to her father.

Neither is Alison, whom Molly attempts to stand up for when she offers to wash Pete's tunic, arguing that 'he's perfectly capable' (p.99) of doing it himself. Bill pits his will directly against Molly's when he steps in to instruct his wife in no uncertain terms to 'wash the lad's tunic' and 'give us dinner' (p.100). Alison, knowing the consequences for disobedience, does as she is told.

Key vocabulary

Clemmed: suffering from hunger.

Hummock: a small knoll or mound.

Kecks: trousers; pants.

Middens: in prehistoric times, sites where domestic waste was disposed.

Q Why is it so important to Bill that Alison, rather than Pete, washes the tunic?

Q What is the significance of the Victorian girl's boot the men find in the bog?

Day Five (pp.104–18)

Summary: *The Professor returns from a visit to town with mysterious 'supplies' (p.105). Silvie, Molly and Dan go foraging, while Pete joins the older men hunting. Later, the men start building a ghost wall. After an argument with Bill, Molly leaves the group to head into town. Alison goes to bed early but the others stay up, drumming and chanting before the ghost wall.*

The discord between Bill and Molly reaches a climax in this section. Already displeased by her refusal to fall happily in with his plans and preferences, and irritated by her attempt to relieve Alison of domestic duties by arguing that Pete should wash his own tunic, for Bill the final straw is Molly's mockery of their ghost wall. Silvie instantly recognises the danger, thinking, 'don't laugh at him, it won't be you who catches it, don't make him feel stupid' (p.110). Reviving a previous topic of contention, he snaps at Molly when she refers to her 'delicate disposition', commenting that 'picky lasses went hungry … it weren't for the likes of you to say who gets what' (p.110).

Molly, fed up, tells Silvie that her father is 'a right chauvinist pig' (p.111) but Silvie defends him, reminding Molly that, unlike the Professor, Bill has seldom had the opportunity to pursue his interests as he can at the camp. This generosity of understanding and attempt to excuse Bill's behaviour are reminiscent of Alison's long-suffering patience with her husband's bullying. They have learned, from Bill, to shift the blame for his moods and violence from him to others.

That evening, Molly leaves the camp to go into town. Bill's open animosity towards her is evident in his declaration to her retreating back: 'spoilt little bitch' (p.114). Alison retires to bed early, leaving Silvie as the sole female member of the group to join in with setting up the ghost wall, as well as the subsequent beating on rabbit-skin drums and chanting to the 'bone-faces' (p.117). Though she describes the evening's events as 'mad play' (p.117), she acknowledges that their singing of death nevertheless 'felt true' (p.118), demonstrating the power of the group to subsume or overcome individual inclinations and suggesting that Silvie, as much as the men, is susceptible to the pull of communal will.

Key point

Pete's decision to go with the men on a 'mission of violence against the local fauna' (p.106) rather than join Silvie, Molly and Dan foraging marks a turning point in his relationships with the others in the camp. Dan has consistently demonstrated a greater capacity for tenderness than Pete – it is he who offers to joint the rabbits to spare Silvie and Molly the task, for example. But Pete has sided with the other young people in treating the camp as an amusing pastime rather than a serious experiment until this point, when he aligns himself with the men and voluntarily chooses to take on the job of killing animals, a task associated with the men, rather than foraging, a more female- and juvenile-coded activity.

Key vocabulary

Cist: a prehistoric stone tomb or place in which sacred objects were kept.

Memento mori: a Latin term meaning 'a reminder of death'.

Palisade: a defensive fence.

Swallows and Amazons*:* a children's novel in which the outdoor adventures of a group of young people include separating into two tribes – the Swallows and the Amazons.

Tacitus: a well-known Roman historian and politician.

Votive objects: objects offered to gods or goddesses in religious rituals.

Q Why do you think Silvie chooses to remain with the men rather than going to bed with Alison?

Q Do you think it is true that Molly 'couldn't see what it was like for us' (p.113), as Silvie believes? Why or why not?

Day Six (pp.119–26)

Summary: *Molly tells Silvie she visited Trudi the previous day, and went out drinking with a boy. She talks to Silvie about her father's abuse but Silvie denies being afraid of him.*

Most of the camp's inhabitants sleep in after their night by the ghost wall. Alison observes to Silvie that the 'sun must've been up again time you and him come in' (p.119), suggesting that what took place there was transporting and exhilarating enough for them to forego sleep. Though in the cold light of day Silvie expects the men to be embarrassed at their wild behaviour the previous night, they are not, calling it a 'great evening' (p.120). The 'strange male back-slapping move, like gorillas' (p.120) that Bill and the Professor exchange implies a new connection between them, a bonding based on their shared reacquaintance with their primitive natures as a result of the night by the wall.

Molly similarly exhibits no remorse for her own defiant behaviour the previous night. But she is unsettled by the ghost wall, calling it 'creepy' (p.122). If she had previously been scornful of the men's 'playing' (p.87), the reality of the wall troubles her, since it suggests the men have already taken things much further than she had anticipated. She asks Silvie if she is 'really OK' with the wall, or if she might be 'scared', but Silvie denies it, confessing to finding it 'interesting' (p.123).

Silvie is also unwilling to admit to being scared of her father when Molly questions her about the marks on her legs. Demonstrating the warped logic her father has instilled in her, she accuses Molly (in her mind) of being 'jealous' that her own father left her and didn't 'care enough to teach [her] a lesson' (p.126). Bill has trained Silvie to conflate love with physical punishment, laying the disturbing groundwork for Silvie's acceptance of the torture she will acquiesce to the following day.

Key vocabulary

Naff: British slang for 'tacky' or 'of low value'.

Q Molly tells Silvie that she and Alison 'had a bit of a giggle' (p.124) when they overheard the sounds of the group at the ghost wall. What does this suggest about how their relationship has developed over the course of the camp?

Day Seven (pp.127–49)

Summary: *The students and Silvie go foraging again; Silvie is separated from the others, who head into town to buy food and alcohol. Bill beats Alison for letting the fire go out. The Professor asks Silvie to take part in a re-enactment of a sacrificial ritual and, at her father's insistence, she agrees. Molly objects strongly and leaves the camp before it takes place. The men bind Silvie and lead her to the bog, where they beat her badly. She is rescued by police, whom Molly, with Trudi, has summoned. Bill is arrested; Silvie and Molly spend the night at Trudi's place.*

In the final chapter, the tensions and divisions within the group culminate in the shocking re-enactment of a sacrifical ritual, during which the men's play-acting turns terrifyingly real. As Silvie puts it, 'they wanted to kill me at sunset' (p.136), though when she is asked to take part in this ritual, the Professor assures her that they 'won't actually hurt you' (p.136), a promise he will spectacularly break.

Molly is outraged to hear of the plan to 'pretend to kill' Silvie, calling it 'insane' (p.139). She urges her to refuse, even offering to shoulder responsibility for the refusal, secure in the knowledge that 'they won't do anything to me' (p.139). But the same cannot be said for Silvie. She knows, from her own and her mother's bitter experience, 'the marks you get if you resist', and decides, in the same fatalistic manner modelled by her mother, that it is better 'just to take what's coming to you anyway' (p.141). She still believes, or tries to, that no physical harm will come to her, though the psychological torment is painful: 'I wish my father didn't want to put a rope around my neck' (p.140).

Molly leaves the camp before the rope is tied around Silvie's neck and she is led, stumbling, to the bog. The Professor's camera and Pete's grin testify to the men's excitement. Silvie resolves to endure the ordeal with the stoicism and acceptance of the murdered bog people; when her father takes out his hunting knife, she recalls the relish with which he had previously described the torture of the bog-girl, cut 'here and here, just done for the pain like' (p.144). Violence from Bill is nothing new and she meets his gaze squarely, but the involvement of the others when they come at her with sticks and stones is a true betrayal.

The episode indicates that the middle-class backgrounds and higher education of the Professor, Dan and Pete are a thin veneer over the same sorts of animalistic and brutal urges in which Bill regularly allows himself to indulge. Though Dan does absent himself before Silvie is physically attacked, he is prepared to see her bound and humiliated, and to join in the drumming that helped to whip up the men into the frenzied state in which they hurt her.

Though Silvie is relieved to be rescued by Molly, Trudi and the police officers, and consoled by Trudi's practical kindness and Molly's tenderness, she is still unable, after everything, to reject her father completely. Instead she feels it is '[her] fault' (p.144) that he is arrested, and she declines to see a doctor, telling Trudi 'he's my dad' (p.147). This reflects the thoroughness of the conditioning by her father. However, the novel ends on a cautiously hopeful note, with Bill safely elsewhere and Silvie in the care of the two strong, compassionate women.

Key point

The first person Molly contacts when she is worried about Silvie is her own mother, who is able to do what Silvie's mother cannot: initiate the involvement of authorities who can help free Silvie from her abusive home.

Key vocabulary

Gill: a unit of measurement of liquid, approximately equal to 0.12 litres.

Picts: early inhabitants of what is now Scotland.

Potash: potassium-bearing minerals or compounds, once created from ashes mixed with water (hence pot + ash) and often used as a fertiliser.

Q What is the significance of the crown that Silvie makes for Molly?

Q It is not made clear who exactly does what to Silvie during the ritual. What does this suggest about who is culpable for the attack?

Q How do you think Alison might react to Bill being arrested? What makes you think this?

CHARACTERS & RELATIONSHIPS

Silvie Hampton

Key quotes

'*CV*, I thought, and felt a thrill of fear, the backwash of my desperation to have such a thing, to leave childhood and dependence behind me, to enter the world.' (p.29)

'In company, I risked it, wanted him to know I still had a mind and a voice.' (pp.75–6)

Seventeen-year-old Silvie's full name is Sulevia, which, her father has told her, he chose for her because it is the name of an Ancient British goddess. However, the students let her know that the name is 'not really British' but only a version of Sylvia, which means 'of the woods' in Latin (p.20).

Silvie lives with her father, Bill, and mother, Alison, in the north of England. She is naturally intelligent and curious, as shown by her knowledge of the natural world and her reflections on the differences between herself and the students, particularly Molly. However, these innate qualities have been tamped down by her opinionated and controlling father, who leaves her little room to express her own thoughts and feelings, and can be brutal when he senses that these differ from his own. Though she is bright and capable, she lacks confidence due to a lifetime of control and criticism from her father, who calls her names such as 'lummock' (p.39) and accuses her of being 'thick' (p.76). Such treatment has taught her passivity and a fear of asserting herself: she repeatedly chastises herself for being a 'know-it-all' (p.28, p.53), afraid that the others will think her 'bossy' (p.28). Though she is in many ways more capable than the students, she lacks the confidence that their privilege has given them, viewing them as 'older and braver' (p.57) than she is, despite the fact that she has endured far more hardship.

Silvie is largely obedient to her parents, but she is not without a rebellious streak. She argues her case to be allowed to bring tampons on the trip, despite her father's objections, and, though she does so nervously, she joins in with some of Molly's rule violations, such as eating fruit pastilles and visiting the Spar. Her tendency to 'provoke' (p.64) her father earns her regular beatings, but these are not sufficient to entirely eliminate her spark of self-belief, nor are they enough to eliminate her love for both the father who hurts her and the mother who is unable to prevent it.

Bill Hampton

Key quotes

'… he likes the idea that there's some original Britishness somewhere, that if he goes back far enough he'll find someone who wasn't a foreigner.' (Pete, p.20)

'… of course he gets het up, stuck behind the wheel all day, a man like that, wanting to be outdoors, he weren't meant for it and it's a crying shame.' (Alison, p.94)

'… don't laugh at him, it won't be you who catches it, don't make him feel stupid.' (Silvie, p.110)

Silvie's father, Bill, works as a bus driver, but his true passion is history – in particular, the Iron Age in Britain. He is an autodidact (self-taught person) who has spent many years reading widely on the subject and exploring the natural world, with a focus on utilising its resources in ways similar to those of the Iron Age Britons.

This interest in history is underpinned by a fierce nostalgia for a time when, as Bill sees it, humans were more resilient, resourceful and capable. Importantly, he also views the Iron Age as a period when the inhabitants of Great Britain were more 'purely' British, before waves of immigration changed the ethnic and cultural landscape of the nation. Essentially he is racist, as he demonstrates with his preference for using 'a more offensive term' (p.24) to refer to dark-skinned people, and his steering his daughter away from 'Paki muck' (p.25) and towards fish and chips on a previous camping trip.

However, this earlier trip, and others on which he took Silvie as a younger child, reveal a softer side to Bill. He is capable of tenderness towards his daughter; she recalls the 'dawn companionship' the pair 'often shared' when she was young (p.71) and, after she fell into a bog on one of their outdoor expeditions, he 'took [her] hand, then, most of the way down, steered [her] around thorns and even cowpats' (p.99), indicating strong feelings of protectiveness towards his only child. Silvie acknowledges that he loves her deeply, recognising that she is his 'votive object' (p.105), the precious item he would sacrifice to the bog if needed. However, his love is of the possessive kind, and he is more concerned with raising Silvie in his image and to share his beliefs than with allowing her to become her own fully realised and autonomous self.

But Bill is not merely domineering. He also exhibits cruelty and sadism, taking great pleasure, for example, in describing in detail how to skin a rabbit: 'peel it like a banana' (p.66). Silvie recognises this quality in her father, and despises it as much as she fears it. Her tone is contemptuous when she notes that her father would love to eat the rabbits whole, their 'small pink bodies skewered over the flames' (p.73), or that he would relish having her and Molly wash their hair with cow urine. She tells the other students frankly that her father is 'a show-off and given to brutality' (p.68) and, although she denies to Molly that she is scared of him, she expends considerable energy trying to 'placate' him (p.111) so that he doesn't 'lose it' (p.78).

Bill's cruelty stems at least partly from insecurity. Silvie notes that some days when he receives his semi-regular missives from his archaeologist friends, his mood plummets, perhaps at 'the thought of those other men who were paid to walk the places Dad loved and write the ideas he could have had' (p.93). His bullying behaviour is thus a misguided and contemptible attempt to command some measure of power over and respect from others.

Key point

Bill recognises that his hold on Silvie is precarious, for all his controlling ways. This is why he tries to limit her contact with the wider world, forbidding her from getting a job and discouraging her from travelling beyond their own part of the country, lest she be exposed to new ideas and other ways of living, and escape his grasp.

Alison Hampton

Key quotes

'Mum didn't believe in fun.' (p.32)

'Mum often spoke of sitting down as a goal, a prize she might win by hard work, but so rarely achieved that the appeal remained unclear to me.' (p.42)

'Obviously Mum was not interested in things, never had been, you only had to look at her to see that.' (p.112)

Silvie's mother, Alison, works as a cashier in a supermarket, where, although she is seated, she is still not truly able to meet 'whatever need was meant by "sitting down"' (p.42). Both at home and at the camp, Alison's daily life is dominated by domestic duties, which she conducts under the close supervision of her husband, Bill.

If Alison is unhappy with her husband's tyranny, she does not express it. She accepts the restrictions her husband places upon her, such as his refusal to have a dishwasher or a sofa in the house, despite the extra work and discomfort this creates for her. In fact, she expresses sympathy and compassion for him, attributing his cruelty to the fact that his job keeps him confined when he was made for the outdoors. Her attitude is 'mustn't grumble, can't be helped, nothing to be gained by making a fuss' (p.47), and she tries to instil this same acceptance in Silvie. She warns her not to 'wind him up' (p.64), knowing that this will result in Silvie being beaten. Alison's love for her daughter is evident in such small gestures as the blanket she folds around her shoulders the night

Silvie stays up with the men while they drum and chant, and the change she lets her keep when Silvie goes to the shop, since Bill won't allow her to earn money of her own. But Alison is not able to prevent Bill's abuse of either her or Silvie.

Significantly, her reaction to Silvie's torture at the bog and Bill's subsequent arrest is not depicted in the novel, leaving the reader to guess whether this dramatic turn of events might free her from her abusive marriage or whether her loyalty to her husband might withstand even this.

Professor Jim Slade

Key quotes

'... as if he couldn't imagine that there were circumstances in which qualities other than being posh and having read a lot might put a person in charge of everyone else.' (p.17)

'... one of the things you learn in my line of work is that there's no steady increase in rationalism over the centuries, it's a mistake to think that they had primitive minds and we don't.' (p.44)

Professor Slade, whom Silvie refers to as 'the Prof', is the person officially in charge of the camp. However, his mild manner and polite tolerance of views that do not accord with his own mean that he is ultimately no match for Bill's strident conviction in his own beliefs. Nor is he able, finally, to resist Bill's appeal to his baser, animal nature when it comes to the ritual sacrifice re-enactment. The Professor's passion for history is excited by the prospect but so, too, is a deeper and mostly repressed aspect of his character, linked to his masculinity and authoritative status in the world beyond the camp.

The Professor is self-absorbed, keen to follow his own interests but apparently little concerned about the inner lives or wellbeing of those with whom he is temporarily living. In explaining why they have chosen Silvie as the 'sacrifice' in the ritual re-enactment, the Professor says that he can't ask Molly, as she is a student and he doesn't want her 'saying she was pressured into anything she didn't want to do' (p.137). He spares no thought for what it might be like to be the person bound and led to a virtual death but is concerned only about any potential repercussions for himself.

The Professor has a wife and two daughters, whom he barely mentions while on camp, suggesting that for him, the experience is quite separate from his 'real' life at home and at work. This compartmentalisation makes it easier for him to allow his customary politeness and reserve to break down, to ultimately reveal a much darker and baser side to his personality.

Molly

Key quotes

'… I just think a lot of it's boys playing in the woods.' (p.87)

'Stay with me, OK, she said, just stay near me and I won't let them do anything, I promise.' (p.139)

When Silvie sees Molly on the morning of their first full day at the camp, her attention is immediately drawn to the details of Molly's appearance that mark her as someone comfortable in her own skin and with a secure sense of her own identity. Though she wears the same rough tunic as the other campers, Molly asserts her individuality with the CND (Campaign for Nuclear Disarmament) badge she affixes to it and the red plastic cherry hair ties with which she secures her plaits.

These adornments reflect Molly's approach to the camping expedition. She is taking part because she likes 'the idea that you can learn from doing things, that it's not all books and speculation' (p.87) and she is mostly willing to accept the restrictions imposed by Bill and, to a lesser extent, the Professor, at least initially. But she is also unwilling to compromise her own beliefs or tamp down her personality in order to accommodate them.

Like Dan and Pete, Molly lives a life of relative privilege compared to Silvie. This is evident in her ignorance of the geography of the north of England, her mimicking of Silvie and her family's northern accents, and her frank surprise at Bill's interest in history given that he is a bus driver. However, she is both principled and tender-hearted, with a strong sense of justice, and she is unafraid to stand up for both Alison and Silvie when she witnesses Bill's mistreatment of them.

Of the three students, it is Molly who fascinates Silvie the most, partly due to her apparent fearlessness and her kindness towards Silvie, but also because Silvie finds herself increasingly attracted to her physically. Their friendship develops over the course of the camp to the point that it is Molly who ultimately saves Silvie from the ritual torture, and Molly in whose arms she finally finds comfort.

Dan

Key quotes

'… he kept going as if he knew what he was doing and the rest of us kept following him.' (pp.21–2)

'I'm not gonna puke, I'm not gonna puke, think about Gran's roses.' (p.66)

Dan is one of the two male students taking part in the camp. Like the other students, he is educated, confident and secure in himself, adapting to the difficulties of camp life with little complaint and willing to learn what he can from the experiment. Despite his lack of experience in hunting and gathering, he takes the lead on their first day of foraging, his self-assurance prompting the others to follow him without question. When Silvie suggests they look for bilberries, he is quick to correct her – 'oh, you mean blueberries' (p.22) – revealing both his ignorance about foraging and his paradoxical confidence in his own knowledge and abilities.

Unlike Silvie's father, however, Dan is willing to acknowledge Silvie's superior survival skills and happy to take her advice. In response to his plan to swim as soon as they reach the beach on their second day of foraging, she points out that he'll need to walk half a mile first as the tide is out. He takes the correction in good humour, saying, 'rub it in why don't you' (p.53). This mild sarcasm is typical of Dan's sense of humour, which occasionally offends Molly, particularly when she feels he is being sexist. She bluntly rebukes him for his comment about girls 'always thinking about where to pee' (p.54), pointing out that 'it's no harder for girls to pee than boys, the problem isn't biology, it's men's fear of women's bodies' (p.55). Again, Dan is able to receive the remonstration without defensiveness, though his excuse that he was only 'joking' so Molly shouldn't 'get upset' (p.55) does not pacify her, since his joke relies on a notion of women as inferior to men. Moreover, his excuse suggests a preference for avoiding conflict rather than genuine engagement with her argument.

This avoidance of conflict is similarly evident in Dan's response to the staging of the sacrificial ritual. Though he repeatedly expresses concern for Silvie's welfare, he does not challenge the other men or take any decisive action to protect or help her. Rather, he simply opts to leave, thus relieving himself of the burden of standing up against injustice and bullying. Like his vomiting at the skinning of the rabbits, which he covers up with leaves, his distaste for the ritual re-enactment appears to stem from a selfish kind of squeamishness rather than any sincere compassion for another vulnerable living creature.

Key point

There are parallels between Alison and Dan in terms of their inability to take action to prevent harm coming to Silvie, despite neither of them wishing her any ill. Alison, though, is cowed by the threat of her husband's brutality. Dan lacks this excuse for his own inaction.

Pete

Key quotes

'You know it's not really British, right? I mean, Sulevia, it's obviously just a version of Sylvia which means – *of the woods* in Latin …' (p.20)

'… I saw a stick in that boy's hand.
Pete, I said, that was Pete …' (p.146)

Like Dan, Pete is not unduly troubled by the deprivations of camp life, willing enough to join in with whatever tasks he is assigned by Bill or the Professor and impressing Silvie with the gusto with which he eats the unappetising gruel Alison makes for breakfast.

He is friendly with Silvie, willing to listen to her advice about foraging and the outdoors. When Dan and Molly argue about Dan's sexism at the beach, Pete defuses the situation with humour and distraction: 'children, children … do you think the sea's actually out there or are we just walking to Norway?' (p.55). With Dan, he relieves Silvie of the burden of jointing the rabbits, allowing her to escape the camp for a while with Molly, despite the fact that he 'nearly vommed' at the skinning process (p.67).

However, Pete shows some early signs of the susceptibility to be carried away by power and seduced by violence that he ultimately displays. At the beach, it is he and not Dan who keeps 'glancing away and then back and then away again' (p.56) at Molly's half-naked body, suggesting a covert and perhaps prurient fascination with her form, reminiscent of Bill's excessive surveillance of his daughter's sexuality. When he opts to join Bill and the Professor on one of their hunting trips, despite his earlier distaste for the dead rabbits, the implication is that he, far more than Dan, has been toughened by their outdoor experiment, and that he is prepared to learn from the example of the older men. Ultimately, this leads to him wielding the stick with which he injures Silvie at the sacrificial ritual.

Key point

Throughout most of the novel, Dan and Pete are characterised similarly; their attitudes and behaviours are mainly in accord. But at the climax of the text, when Silvie is compelled to take part in the sacrificial ritual, they exhibit very different responses to her plight. Dan repeatedly checks on her welfare, asking if she is 'really OK' and 'all right' (p.142). Pete, however, carried away by the momentum of the group, 'grin[s]' at the prospect of her sacrifice and joins in Silvie's torture – afterwards, Silvie recalls that he had a stick in his hand, while Dan 'left, quite early' (p.146). In so doing, Dan reveals his moral qualms about the situation, and exhibits a degree of courage in removing himself from the setting. However, his bravery does not extend to standing up for or actively helping Silvie. In this sense he might be thought of as a typical bystander, disapproving of the others' behaviour but unwilling to put himself at risk to prevent it. Pete, meanwhile, is thoroughly corrupted by the charged atmosphere and the example of his elders. Though he previously exhibited no animosity towards Silvie and in fact seemed to regard her fondly, he is willing to go along with the group to the extent of physically hurting her.

Trudi Kelley

Key quotes

'Why are you sorry ...' (p.82)

'Here we go then, let's get those cuts covered, shall we.' (p.148)

Trudi is a minor character, yet she plays a pivotal role in *Ghost Wall*. One of very few representatives of the world beyond the camp, she offers assistance to Silvie and Molly should they need it, and keeps her word, coming to Silvie's aid the night she is attacked. Her kind and capable nature provides Silvie with yet another example of admirable womanhood; even the white streaks in her hair are 'purposeful' (p.82). Like Molly, Trudi is not afraid of men and in fact is inclined to ridicule their masculine posturing, as in the conversation she and Molly have about men's reluctance to ask for directions.

When she takes in Silvie after the ritual re-enactment, Trudi encourages her to see a doctor but respects her refusal, understanding her reluctance and the vestiges of loyalty she retains to her father – 'he's my dad' (p.147), Silvie tells her – to a greater extent than Molly is able to, demonstrating her sensitivity and wisdom.

Key point

Trudi's interest in Roman history and the natural environment provides a counterpoint to that of the men in the novel. She offers Molly and Silvie 'advice about plants' (p.84) and recognises that it must be harder for them to forage than it would have been for prehistoric people due to the farming of the land, a point never acknowledged by Bill or the Professor. Trudi wears her knowledge lightly, offering it without imposing it on the young women, and she is critical of men's general inability or unwillingness to 'admit uncertainty' (p.84).

THEMES, IDEAS & VALUES

Coming of age

Key quotes

'… the adolescence I couldn't wait to leave.' (p.21)

'When I grow up, I thought, when I get away, I will go out and buy myself pants in emerald and turquoise and scarlet … I will have lipstick and thin tights and high heels …' (p.59)

At seventeen, Silvie is on the verge of adulthood, yet the control her father wields over her means that in many ways her development is delayed. Though she dreams of escape and a life beyond her home, she finds it difficult to conceive that such things might truly be possible. But her exposure to the students at the camp – 'the three older and braver' than she is (p.57) – broadens Silvie's horizons in many ways. When she hears them talk about travel, her mind snags on the practical details; she wonders, 'how do you get to Berlin, can you start at the bus stop, do you take an aeroplane or the train, several trains?' (p.16). The mention of so ordinary an item as a CV invokes a 'thrill of fear' (p.29) in Silvie as she imagines what it might be like to 'enter the world' beyond her claustrophobic home. The casual entitlement the students evince towards such privileges as education, travel and a career illuminates Silvie's own lack of autonomy in new and unsettling ways.

Silvie's growing friendship with Molly provides her with an example of womanhood far removed from the traditional subservient role her father tries to shape her for, and which her mother, Alison, exemplifies. Molly is outspoken and fearless – demonstrated, for example, when she raises her fingers at two boys in a car who shout at her and Silvie as they walk to the Spar 'as if there were no possible consequences for a girl making obscene gestures on the public highway' (p.80).

Silvie's relationship with Molly also awakens her latent sexuality. Silvie is fascinated by Molly's physical form, her gaze lingering on the details of Molly's purple underwear, the 'pale hair poking through the lace of the pants', and the pale belly Silvie 'wanted to touch' (p.56) when Molly undresses to swim at the beach. Molly's tenderness towards Silvie is repeatedly linked to the softness of her body, as when she offers Silvie her hand after Silvie stumbles over a branch while they are out foraging together, or strokes Silvie's hair as she tries to persuade her not to cooperate with the ritual re-enactment. It is Molly who ultimately rescues Silvie from this dangerous and humiliating procedure, and Molly's body in which Silvie again seeks comfort once the pair are safely at Trudi's house, with Molly reassuring her that, both symbolically and physically, she is placing herself 'between you and everything else' (p.148). This supportive and healthy relationship represents the distance Silvie has come from the downtrodden, lonely girl she was at the beginning of the camp.

Gender roles

Key quotes

'Because they are men, I thought, because they're in charge, because there will be consequences if you don't [take them seriously].' (p.88)

'I ... wanted to go on believing that men were also people, that there are not, in fact, two kinds of human.' (p.96)

The two older men among the group of campers, Bill and Professor Slade, assume a natural authority. The Professor is the organiser of the group and accustomed to deference from his students. He begins by taking charge, assigning the campers duties on their first day. However, Bill is quick to assert his own authority, taking the lead in the skinning of the rabbits, for example, and overseeing Alison's preparation of their meals.

Alison's confinement to the roundhouse and domestic duties reflects Bill's belief in traditional roles for men and women: the men engage in physical pursuits such as hunting, and in intellectual pursuits such as the study of history. Women, however, and particularly wives, are duty-bound to suppress their own interests and desires in order to serve men. Although Silvie might seem to enjoy more freedom than her mother, Bill keeps just as careful supervision of her. Since she was a child, she has been permitted to join him on outdoor excursions and museum visits, but her role is strictly that of obedient pupil and audience for his opinions. She is allowed to join the students on their foraging missions, but only at Bill's instruction, and he also makes sure she helps her mother with the cooking and cleaning, training her from a young age to accept what he views as her natural place within the home. For the same reason, he discourages further education or travel.

Molly, however, provides a very different example of womanhood for Silvie, hence Bill's strong dislike of her. Bold and strong-willed, she refuses to be reduced to a stereotype of femininity. She encourages Silvie to stand up to her father and Alison to resist the role of servant she has been assigned, like when she tells her not to wash Pete's tunic, or invites her on a walk. But both Silvie and Alison have been so abused by Bill that they are unable to follow Molly's example. Silvie's consumption of a forbidden fruit pastille and Alison's shared giggle with Molly about the ghost wall celebrations are the most either can manage in terms of rebellion against his iron rule.

It is not incidental that Silvie's attackers during the ritual are all men, and that her rescue is instigated by women. Though during the camp both Dan and Pete have demonstrated some concern for her welfare, recognising the brutality of her father, ultimately she cannot rely on them for help when she is in real danger. Indeed, they each, to varying degrees, play a role in putting her in that position. Their attack on her can be seen as an extension of the 'war-games' (p.108) they have begun to engage in, which Molly recognises as an expression of the masculine desire for power and conquest. Like Trudi, Molly is scornful of such activities, and her disillusionment with the way the camp has been hijacked by the men for their own atavistic (outmoded) purposes leads her to increasingly break the rules and absent herself from it. When Molly, her mother and Trudi arrange for Silvie to be rescued from her torture, they invert the classic trope of the maiden being rescued by a prince and demonstrate that the segregated world in which Bill (and possibly, secretly, the other men) would like to reside is no longer possible.

Nostalgia

Key quotes

'That's where you come from, those folk, that's how it used to be.' (p.39)

'He wanted his own ancestry, wanted a lineage, a claim on something.' (p.45)

Ghost Wall presents a warning about the dangers of nostalgia, particularly when the impetus is dissatisfaction with the state of the world and personal disappointment or disillusionment. Bill, in particular, is drawn to a mythical past in which Britain was racially pure, and his own talents and qualities – for instance, a propensity for violence – would have been useful, even valorised, rather than criticised or criminalised, as in the modern world. But looking back on the past can only ever offer an impressionistic view of 'how things were', partly because we can only access limited evidence about how people lived in the distant past and partly because the perspectives of the marginalised or powerless are missing or partial amid that evidence.

For example, the sacrificed bog people cannot articulate how they felt about their experiences; though they show no signs of defensive wounds, modern historians cannot tell if they went willingly to their deaths or were perhaps drugged to ensure their compliance. Molly points out that Iron Age women likely would not have enjoyed the same freedoms as men, obliged to spend their time 'foraging and cooking so the men could play' (p.124).

Key point

The Professor argues that overlaying modern thinking on past peoples is inaccurate and dangerous. He suggests it is presumptuous to assume that past civilisations were only less evolved versions of present ones, or that they would have necessarily shared modern understandings of the world – he argues, for example, that the significance of Hadrian's Wall for the Romans was very different from the significance of the Berlin Wall for twentieth-century Germans. Moreover, romanticising the past requires overlooking its limitations and ignoring the advantages associated with the present. The Professor notes that Iron Age Britons 'didn't even live long enough to die of cancer' (p.42), while Molly points out that 'people have been dying of cholera and dysentery for centuries' (p.74). Thus Bill's idea of the Iron Age as a sort of golden age for Britain is both inaccurate and self-serving, endorsing his idea of himself as strong, resourceful and a natural leader, whose inability to achieve the respect and success he believes he is owed is due to the failings of the time in which he lives, rather than his personal inadequacies.

Borders

Key quotes

'… on the edge of the water-earth, in the time and space between life and death …' (p.3)

'… we were still on it, out on England's blurred margins.' (p.54)

'They weren't dead, the bog people, not to those who'd killed them.' (p.104)

Borders and boundaries of many kinds, including physical, temporal, emotional and liminal, are a key feature of *Ghost Wall*. The novel highlights the porosity and insecurity of these boundaries, suggesting that situations or states usually understood to be fixed opposites, such as life and death, might be closer than generally assumed.

Physical borders

As an island nation, the UK's physical boundary is the ocean in which the students swim. But, as Silvie notes:

> You'd think a coastline more definite than a land border but it's not so, not when you walk the watery edge at the turn of the tide and cannot say if you are on dry land, exactly. (p.54)

Moreover, at low tide the beach they visit 'looked more like a desert' (p.53), leading Silvie to reflect that once this area had been joined to Denmark, that there had been human settlements under what is now the North Sea. Thus time and rising sea levels created a physical border between England and the European continent that had previously not existed, and the continuing action of the tides reminds contemporary inhabitants of Britain that neither land nor sea, continent nor island, is permanent. Archaeological discoveries of 'carved figurines … brooches and buttons' (p.53) continue the intrusion of the distant past into the present.

Like the sea that can seem a desert, the Northumbrian bogs also occupy more than one state, being both water and earth. They, too, retain objects once dear to prehistoric occupants of the area, 'murdered things' (p.103) sacrificed to the bogs just as certain chosen people had been. Silvie recalls a book her father had shown her that suggested that both the objects and the people given to the bogs 'would have lain there, dead and still present' (p.103) after their immersion, a paradoxical state that allowed their value to their communities to outlast their lives.

Walls, another form of physical border, are also shown to be both enduring yet breachable. The group camps near Hadrian's Wall, which was once around 117 kilometres in length and at least 3.7 metres high, but of which little remains today. Despite its physical diminution, however, it remains historically and symbolically important: Bill and Silvie walk the length of it in a kind of pilgrimage, and for Bill it remains an important indication that the ancient Britons had sufficient might to 'put the wind up' (p.44) the Romans who built it. Similarly, the ghost wall built by the male campers in homage to similar prehistoric ghost walls carries a talismanic power far exceeding its physical capacity as a barricade.

Even skin is permeable, despite Bill's assurances that bog water 'won't go further nor skin' (p.98). Silvie knows this to be untrue, that it will 'fill the inner skins of every orifice' (p.98), and the bog people's wounds – and Silvie's eventual ones – prove skin to be of little use as protection.

Temporal borders

Ghost Wall also suggests that the past and the present co-exist. The living and the dead continue to communicate across the passage of time: as basket-weaver Louise puts it, 'I'm always trying to do what dead people tell me' (p.34). Equally, as Silvie reflects, the long deceased likely 'imagined us first, maybe we were conjured out of the deep past by other minds' (p.34). She feels that the campers are as much ghosts as the dead, whose actions and behaviours they are mimicking in an effort to understand them better. The dead address the living in their own ways, through artefacts discovered by archaeologists, such as the 'brooches and buttons' (p.53) found in what was once Doggerland (the area of land that once connected Britain to continental Europe), and by casual explorers, such as the Victorian girl's boot found by Bill, the Professor and Pete in a bog. The bog people of many centuries earlier also tell their own stories to contemporary peoples through the marks on their bodies.

Key point

The continuing power of the skulls of the dead attests to the ongoing commerce between the past and the present, the living and the dead. The Iron Age Britons built ghost walls of human skulls to terrify their enemies, but also kept the skulls of family members close, sometimes within their own homes, as though death was no barrier to their influence over and involvement in the lives of others. Meanwhile, in a contemporary setting, the continuing relevance and interest of history in the present is expressed in children's games that re-imagine historical battles, such as those between 'cowboys and Indians, Allies and Huns' (p.107).

Emotional borders and liminal states

One of the most troubling and fascinating aspects of the bog people is their grisly and prolonged deaths. Evidence of torture on their preserved bodies suggests that they were kept by their killers in a state close to, and yet not quite, death. Even prior to being taken for sacrifice, they occupied an in-between space; knowing they were marked for death, they 'had weeks or months ... to get used to [their] status as ghost' (p.71).

Silvie herself occupies an in-between state, on the cusp of adulthood and more than ready to reach it, yet held by her father in a kind of extended childhood, prevented from making her own choices or exercising her will. Bill's need for control can also be understood as a failure to recognise natural boundaries. He has trouble understanding and respecting where he ends and his wife and daughter begin, viewing them as extensions of himself, as indicated by his apology to the Professor when they come upon Silvie bathing.

The body

Key quotes

'It was one of my father's themes, the way women allow their inferior plumbing to shape their relationship with the Great Outdoors.' (p.55)

'... I thought, I can't get through today, not like this, it's too sore, it's never been this bad before, but I knew that I could and would. It was not as if there was an alternative.' (p.75)

'Children's bodies were not their own ...' (p.125)

In *Ghost Wall*, the human body in various forms is subjected to deprivation and abuse. Moss shows an interest not only in the limits of physical endurance but also in the capacity that people have for cruelty and the lengths to which they will go in order to exert physical power over one another.

The most extreme example of physical abuse in the novel is that which took place many hundreds of years prior to the contemporary events depicted: the torture and murder of the bog people. But, as the Professor points out, such cruelty is not a relic of history: 'it's a mistake to think that they had primitive minds and we don't' (p.44). Modern humans are as capable of violence as – and arguably often with less reason than – prehistoric humans, who at least were likely acting in accordance with the logic of their particular religious beliefs when it came to their treatment of the bog people. The same cannot be said of the male campers when they elect to re-enact a religious sacrifice with Silvie playing the part of the victim and, despite their assurances that no physical harm will come to her, become so intoxicated by their power that they end up by beating and stabbing her. It is implied that they might have gone even further than this, perhaps to the point of killing her, had Molly not raised the alarm and instigated her just-in-time rescue.

The violence Bill inflicts on Silvie and Alison is another prominent example of the damage humans can inflict on one another. During the camp Silvie suffers a serious beating at his hands, and Alison appears more than once with bruises. These physical marks of harm have parallels with the damage done to the bog people 'for the pain like' (p.144), and it is implied that Bill uses violence not merely as a means of control but also because he derives a sadistic pleasure from it.

Yet *Ghost Wall* does not only dwell on the body's vulnerability to harm. It also celebrates its resilience and capacity to endure: Silvie's wounds heal; the ritual does not kill her. Even the long-dead bog people show an endurance of sorts, their bodies preserved enough to convey something of their story to people many generations removed from them. Similarly, the body parts of the ancestors of Iron Age peoples retain a symbolic power: their skulls are used in the construction of ghost walls and even kept on display in some houses.

Moreover, the body is also shown to be a source of joy and pleasure – less frequently than it is depicted as damaged, perhaps, but finally and triumphantly. The students 'disport' themselves (p.57) with pleasure at the beach, and Silvie finds physical comfort in the muddy pool, where 'the water stroked [her] sunburn, soothed away the itchy sand' (p.60). Ultimately, it is with the tender image of the bodies of Silvie and Molly intertwined that the novel closes.

Groupthink

Key quotes

'Maybe they're just socialized that way and can't help it, poor dears ...' (Trudi, p.84)

'... something that would be really silly if you did it in the street or even on your own ... somehow it's not when everyone joins in.' (p.125)

In its mildest form, groupthink involves a general consensus, often unspoken, to behave or think in certain ways. The camp experiment, during which all participants agree to adopt the false reality that they are living in Iron Age times and therefore must live as prehistoric peoples did, is a relatively benign example of the way in which a group of people can reach a mutual agreement to set aside their society's usual mores or beliefs.

But the climax of the novel, in which Silvie is 'sacrificed', is a formidable demonstration of the way in which the power of the group can absolve individuals of moral responsibility and thus pave the way for extreme and destructive behaviours. While her father has a long history of violence towards her, no other man at the camp exhibits any animosity or aggression towards Silvie before the night of the ritual, nor is there any evidence of their having a history of violent behaviour. In fact, the Professor is characterised as mild-mannered, educated and apparently law-abiding, as suggested by his concern about involving Molly in the ritual lest it cause official repercussions. Yet his love of history is able to be turned to dark ends under Bill's influence. Nor does Bill need to coerce or unduly pressure the Professor to share his penchant for violence. It is the Professor himself who asks Silvie to take the part of the sacrificial victim, despite knowing that it will be at the very least an emotionally disturbing process that he cannot subject a student to. The thrill he displays at the prospect of the construction of the ghost wall and the re-enactment is genuine: he is 'excited, het up' (p.95) about the idea; he returns from buying skulls in town 'whistling' (p.104). Despite his long career in higher education and previous participation in similar trips, he has never before attempted such a project as the re-enactment, suggesting that it requires the influence of another with similar inclinations for his baser instincts to be expressed.

Likewise, Dan and Pete are typical middle-class university students who, for most of the novel, show no tendency towards violence and in fact are inclined to be 'sceptical' (p.120) of the aims of the camp. They have an easy friendship with Molly, are respectful towards Alison and show kindness to Silvie. However, over time, these patterns of behaviour begin to change: from nearly vomiting at the skinning of rabbits, Pete happily joins the older men hunting, while Dan goes from mocking the idea of the wall made with 'ghost rabbits ... with their little teeth' (p.109) to drumming and chanting before it. Even Silvie, who views the 'guys ... playing with big sticks' (p.107) as engaged in some kind of childish game like 'Iron Age cowboys and Indians' (p.108), elects to stay up with the men as they erect the wall. While at first she is only 'wanting to see what happened' (p.115), she is soon caught up in the atmosphere and the communal excitement. She observes that she 'found [her]self joining in' (p.117), as though her will has been hijacked by a greater power.

Ultimately, though, of the students, it is only Pete who is so overcome by the hysteria of the final evening that he is not only able but excited to inflict physical harm on Silvie. It is his character arc that provides the starkest example of the power of the group to override one's individual inclinations and principles, moving as he does from being Silvie's friend and considering Bill a bully – 'is he always like that, Silvie?' (p.68) – to becoming sufficiently enamoured by the older men's display of power over the bound and vulnerable Silvie to raise his own weapon against her.

Power

Key quotes

'Foreigners coming over here, telling us what to think.' (p.45)

'... they just want to kill things and talk about fighting ...' (Molly, p.88)

'My daughter. Break her and stake her to the bog, stop her before she gets away.' (p.104)

The most obvious example of Moss' concern with power relations in *Ghost Wall* is her depiction of the consequences of coercive control within a family. Both Silvie and her mother are victims of Bill's need to exert his dominance and impose his beliefs and preferences on every aspect of their lives, from what they eat to whom they socialise with. But *Ghost Wall* also suggests that this abuse of power in a domestic setting is connected to the abuse of power within larger social systems. Gender, class and race are all dimensions along which people can be divided into the powerful and the powerless, and the novel explores the implications of this for both those who benefit from such divisions and those who are harmed by them.

Power and class

Bill's bullying behaviour towards his family and, to a lesser extent, the students at the camp is both an exercising of his power and a consequence of his lack of it in the wider world. As a working-class bus driver, he lacks the authority that the Professor's education provides him. As Silvie notes, her father's skills are 'redundant except for archaeological purposes' (p.107). Thus the home – and, to an extent, the camp – is one of the few arenas in which Bill can assert control.

Bill is resentful of the class differences between himself and the Professor and students. He describes the south of England (associated with relative privilege compared to the north) as 'just traffic and throngs of people ... everything built over' (p.95) and dismisses Molly as a 'spoilt little bitch' (p.114), the first adjective revealing the connection he is making between her apparent economic privilege and her assertiveness. Silvie, too, becomes aware of class differences during the camp, reflecting that she 'had not understood until meeting the students that we lived "up north", that we were "Northerners"' (p.79). For her, though, the students' relative privilege is enviable for the freedom it allows them: to travel, to pursue higher education, to make their own decisions about their lives. She envies the confidence this instils in them, believing that their economic and social privilege is a shield against pain or hardship; she imagines Molly's 'huge house and garden' (p.112), concluding that this sort of material advantage means that Molly 'couldn't see what it was like for us' (p.113). In fact, Molly too has faced challenges, her father having abandoned the family when she was five. But Silvie, mired in her own misery and no doubt influenced by her father's highly developed resentment towards those better off than he is, struggles to see Molly as anything other than enviably fortunate. And it is clear that Molly's upbringing has in fact kept her somewhat sheltered. Thoughtlessly, though without any malice, she questions why a bus driver would be interested in history and mimics Alison's accent, insensitivities to which Silvie is quick to respond defensively: 'don't laugh at people's accents, you do know yours sounds weird to me, posh' (p.95).

Power and race

Bill's dislike of foreigners stems from a similar source as his mistrust of those more privileged than he is. He rejects the notion that Britons during the Iron Age were mostly of Celtic origin, preferring to imagine that he is the descendant of 'some tribe sprung from English soil like mushrooms in the night' (p.45), and he is openly racist towards contemporary Britons whose heritage does not align with his vision of a racially pure nation. The students are inclined to mock him for this attitude (as does Silvie, albeit silently), reflecting the general association of left-wing, progressive ideologies with young, tertiary-educated Britons, and conservative and even xenophobic attitudes with older, working-class people.

Complicating notions of power

Yet *Ghost Wall* complicates this dichotomy. It is not the case that a straightforward contrast is drawn between Bill's ignorance or lack of enlightenment and the progressive and egalitarian attitude of the students and the Professor. In fact, the latter group are depicted as in many ways oblivious to their own access to power, and how this might shape the ways in which they see the world. Just as Molly displays a casual prejudice towards or ignorance about the working class, so do the male students demonstrate an equivocal attitude towards women's rights, despite superficially seeming supportive. Dan makes sexist jokes, and while Pete tells Alison 'it's no day to be slaving over a hot stove' (p.133), neither he nor Dan relieve her of her domestic chores. Nor do they support Molly when she attempts to stand up for Alison over the washing of Pete's tunic. Their own power is something they take for granted and, when alerted to its existence, seem reluctant to cede, despite their derision of Bill's quest for an 'original Britishness' (p.20). The Professor similarly accepts the respect of others as his due, never questioning the ways in which his gender, race and class might afford him advantages others lack. When he debates with Bill about the ethnic makeup of Iron Age Britons, it is not Bill's implied racism he takes issue with, but his historical inaccuracy.

Key point

Molly's relationship with power is complicated along both gender and class lines. As a young woman, she lacks the physical power to dominate the older men, and Bill openly discriminates against her for violating his traditional notions of femininity. However, she retains a certain amount of power associated with class and economic privilege, as well as the autonomy afforded to most adults, that Silvie, as a still-dependent child, lacks. Molly is able to use these privileges to help Silvie when she most needs it.

DIFFERENT INTERPRETATIONS

Different interpretations arise from different responses to a text. Over time, a text will evoke a wide range of responses from its readers, who may come from various social or cultural groups and live in very different places and historical periods. Responses by critics and reviewers can be published in newspapers, journals and books, both online and in print. They can also be expressed in discussions among readers in the media, classrooms, book groups and so on.

While there is no single correct reading or interpretation of a text, it is important to understand that an interpretation is more than a personal opinion – it is the justification of a point of view on the text. To present an interpretation of a text based on your point of view, you must use a logical argument and support it with relevant evidence from the text.

Critical viewpoints

Ghost Wall received almost universal praise on its release. *The Guardian*'s Sarah Crown calls it 'a short, sharp shock of a book that closes around you like a vice' (Crown 2018). Annalisa Quinn in *The Atlantic* similarly describes it as 'a tiny, sharp knife of a novel' (Quinn 2019), as well as 'acutely lovely', noting its complex examination of the way in which cruelty and power are eternal dynamics underpinning every society throughout time. Dana Hansen, writing in the *Chicago Review of Books,* describes the novel as 'powerful in its tightly controlled prose and multiple understated themes' (Hansen 2019), identifying its concerns with male violence and nationalism as key foci.

Multiple critics, including Hansen and Justine Hyde, writing in *The Sydney Morning Herald,* note the novel's timeliness in terms of its relevance to Brexit. Hansen states the novel 'contains political undertones and motifs relevant to our nationalistic age of walls and border security' (Hansen 2019), while Hyde refers to its depiction of

Bill's nostalgia for a mythical pure British race a 'prescient theme for a post-Brexit Britain' (Hyde 2018).

Its exploration of gender roles and their historical evolution is also noted by critics such as Margaret Talbot, whose review in *The New Yorker* claims that the novel's 'feminism ... felt utterly contemporary' (Talbot 2019) and refers to its 'urgent themes'. Likewise, Hyde considers the novel 'a devastating exploration of how we live' now (Hyde 2018), despite its setting somewhere around the turn of the century, and Hansen sees it as 'a parable for our broken times' (Hansen 2019).

Critics also note the novel's compactness, calling it 'taut' (Hyde 2018), 'compact, riveting' (Hagy 2019) and 'slender' (Talbot 2019), all admiring its ability to evoke a vivid sense of place and explore multiple complex ideas within its brief length. Several critics, among them Crown and Hyde, heralded *Ghost Wall*, at the time of its publication, as marking a turning point in Moss' literary career, predicting wider recognition and further awards for the author (Crown 2018; Hyde 2018).

Two possible interpretations

The following interpretations demonstrate how even directly contrasting viewpoints about a text can be valid, as long as they are supported with evidence from that text.

Interpretation 1: *Ghost Wall* suggests that learning about the past can help us to better understand the present.

The participants in the camp might all exhibit different attitudes towards, and degrees of investment in, their shared project of re-creating life in Iron Age Britain, but all harbour a curiosity about the past and a desire to learn from it in ways that will inform their contemporary lives. While some, such as Bill, might attempt to turn the knowledge they have acquired to negative ends, like promoting a return to a 'purer' Britain that never actually existed, this does not negate the fact that all are ultimately enriched, to varying degrees, by their learning. Indeed, the novel suggests that, even if we derive different understandings of our history, we fail to learn the lessons of the past at our peril.

Ghost Wall suggests that the past is always with us; therefore, to ignore its lessons would be to remain in wilful ignorance. The preserved bog people, who carry their stories into the present day, and the continuing existence of physical objects as large as Hadrian's Wall and as small as brooches and buttons, testify to the multiple ways in which the past continues to communicate meaning to those in the present. For historians like the Professor, these relics give insights into facts about the past. For others, they allow an empathetic act of imagination that places them inside the minds and hearts of those long gone. Basket-weaver Louise, for instance, communes with the dead by using their tools to create the sorts of products they would have made, 'trying to think their thoughts too' (p.34). For Silvie, the discovery of a Victorian girl's boot in a bog allows her to vividly imagine the wearer, and the full and complex life she would once have had: 'where is she now, did she deserve only to lose her shoe ...?' (p.101). Similarly, she is able to put herself in the place of the bog-girl, who 'had slept and woken, had sleepless nights, felt sun and wind and rain' (p.70). This display of compassion and understanding for girls she never knew is one of the reasons Silvie could never engage in the kind of cruelty displayed by both the murderers of the bog people and her own father.

Even Bill's self-interested misreadings of the past are enlightening for what they reveal about the present preoccupations of people like him. Many critics have noted the relevance of the text to a post-Brexit Britain in which a faction of English people still want the country to return to the independent glory it enjoyed during the Empire years, or even, as Bill exemplifies, to a time before this, when some kind of essential Britishness native to the land could be imagined to exist. The Professor points out the error of this sort of thinking, telling Bill that Iron Age Britons 'weren't exactly British ... their identities were tribal' (p.45), just as he points out Bill's mispronunciations. But understanding what Bill is seeking from the past, and the insecurities related to class, race and wealth that prompt his longing, is instructive for his contemporaries, as the students' astute assessment of him – 'he likes the idea that there's some original Britishness somewhere, that if he goes far back enough he'll find someone who wasn't a foreigner' (p.20) – shows.

The one character in the novel who evinces little curiosity about the past is Alison, too browbeaten by her husband to take an independent interest in anything beyond her housewifely obligations. Her failure of imagination in this regard could be understood as being partially responsible for her low state; for instance, she shows little awareness of the rights fought for by previous generations of feminists that women such as Molly and Trudi take for granted.

Thus *Ghost Wall* presents a powerful argument for engaging with the past in order to promote compassion and empathy, and to learn from the mistakes of previous generations in order not to repeat them.

Interpretation 2: *Ghost Wall* depicts the dangers of looking to the past for answers about how to live in the present.

Ghost Wall depicts a disparate group of people with various motives for taking part in the experiential endeavour designed to give them 'a flavour' (p.7) of Iron Age life. The Professor aims to satisfy his own intellectual curiosity, as well as to give his students an educational experience. The students are motivated by the same curiosity as well as a desire for academic credit. Bill Hampton's motivation is to reconnect with a past era he glorifies due to his misperception of it as a time in which Britain was racially 'pure' and Britons were a self-sufficient, brave and resourceful people. It is Bill's approach that most starkly reveals the dangers of looking back to the past for lessons to apply to the present day.

Bill is a keen amateur historian but he is neither a well-educated nor a dispassionate one. He has a romanticised conception of the Iron Age, the period in which he is most interested, and stubbornly clings to his misperceptions in the face of the Professor's corrections, 'lift[ing]' his chin and lock[ing] eyes with the fire' (p.46) without conceding a point during one key discussion. Bill's exploration of the past is self-interested, justifying as it does in his mind his xenophobic attitude, expressed in his offensive language ('Negroes', p.24; 'Paki', p.25) and his lack of curiosity about the world beyond his homeland; he has 'never flown' (p.35). It also feeds his innate sadism, evidenced by the pleasure he takes in the slaughter of animals and the cruelty he inflicts on his daughter during the ritual re-enactment, all in the name of 'play-acting' (p.137) the past. Thus his passion for history only cements his prejudices and resentments, ill-equipping him for success or happiness in the modern world.

Ghost Wall demonstrates that misunderstandings and misuses of history, such as those demonstrated by Bill and, to a lesser extent, the other men, are inevitable, partly because it is impossible to accurately or completely know the past. As Silvie says to the Professor of the sacrificial ritual, 'we don't know, do we ... what it was like, you said there's no evidence' (p.136). Moreover, where evidence from the past does exist, such as the bog bodies, it is open to interpretation: as Bill explains to Silvie, no one knows whether the bog people's lack of defensive wounds means they acquiesced to their violent deaths or were drugged. This uncertainty has dark consequences for Silvie, as Bill and the Professor's fascination with 'want[ing] to try' in order that 'we might learn' (p.136) ultimately results in her physical and emotional torture.

Given the unknowability of the past – even the Professor's extensive knowledge is partial and uncertain, full of hedging phrases such as 'as far as we can tell' and 'seems to be' (p.45) – and the harmful uses to which it can be put, *Ghost Wall* suggests that looking backwards for guidance as to how to live today is at best foolish and at worst downright dangerous.

QUESTIONS & ANSWERS

This section focuses on your own analytical writing on the text, and gives you strategies for producing high-quality responses in your coursework and exam essays.

Essay writing – an overview

An essay on a literary work is a formal and serious piece of writing that presents your point of view on the text, usually in response to a given topic. Your 'point of view' in an essay is your interpretation of the meaning of the text's language, structure, characters, situations and events, supported by detailed analysis of textual evidence.

Analyse – don't summarise

In your essays it is important to avoid simply summarising what happens in a text.

- A **summary** is a description or paraphrase (retelling in different words) of the characters and events. For example: 'Macbeth has a horrifying vision of a dagger dripping with blood before he goes to murder King Duncan.'
- An **analysis** is an explanation of the real meaning or significance that lies 'beneath' the text's words (and images, for a film). For example: 'Macbeth's vision of a bloody dagger shows how deeply uneasy he is about the violent act he is contemplating, and conveys his sense that supernatural forces are impelling him to act.'

A limited amount of summary is sometimes necessary to let your reader know which part of the text you wish to discuss. However, always keep this to a minimum and follow it immediately with your analysis of what this part of the text is really telling us.

Plan your essay

Carefully plan your essay so that you have a clear idea of what you are going to say. The plan ensures that your ideas flow logically, your argument remains consistent and you stay on topic. An essay plan should be a list of **brief dot points** covering no more than half a page.

- Include your central argument or main contention – a concise statement of your overall response to the topic.
- Write three or four dot points for each paragraph, indicating the main idea and evidence/examples from the text. Note that in your essay you will need to *expand* on these points and *analyse* the evidence.

Structure your essay

An essay is a complete, self-contained piece of writing. It has a clear beginning (the introduction), middle (several body paragraphs) and end (the last paragraph or conclusion). It must also have a central argument that runs throughout, linking each paragraph to form a coherent whole. See examples of introductions and conclusions in the 'Analysing a sample topic' and 'Sample answer' sections.

The introduction establishes your overall response to the topic. It includes your main contention and outlines the main evidence you will refer to in the course of the essay. Write your introduction *after* you have done a plan and *before* you write the rest of the essay.

The body paragraphs argue your case – they present evidence from the text and explain how this evidence supports your argument. Each body paragraph needs:

- a strong **topic sentence** (usually the first sentence) that states the main point being made in the paragraph
- **evidence** from the text, including some brief quotations
- analysis of the textual evidence, with **explanation** of its significance and how it supports your argument
- **links back to the topic** in one or more statements, usually towards the end of the paragraph.

Connect the body paragraphs so that your discussion flows smoothly. Use some linking words and phrases such as 'similarly' and 'on the other hand', though don't start every paragraph like this. Another strategy is to use a significant word from the last sentence of one paragraph in the first sentence of the next.

Use key terms from the topic – or synonyms for them – throughout, so the relevance of your discussion to the topic is always clear.

The conclusion ties everything together and finishes the essay. It includes strong statements that emphasise your central argument and provide a clear response to the topic.

Avoid simply restating the points made earlier in the essay – this will end on a very flat note and imply that you have run out of ideas and vocabulary. The conclusion should be a logical extension of what you have written, not just a repetition or summary of it. Writing an effective conclusion can be a challenge. Try using these tips:

- Start by linking back to the final sentence of the second-last paragraph, rather than leaping to your main contention straight away – this helps your writing to flow.
- Use synonyms and expressions with equivalent meanings to vary your vocabulary. This allows you to reinforce your line of argument without being repetitive.
- When planning your essay, think of one or two broad statements or observations about the text's wider meaning. These should be related to the topic and your overall argument. Keep them for the conclusion, since they will give you something 'new' to say but still follow logically from your discussion. The introduction will be focused on the topic, but the conclusion can present a wider view of the text.

Essay topics

1. *Ghost Wall* demonstrates that power always corrupts.
   Do you agree?
2. The men are the villains and the women the heroes of *Ghost Wall*.
   To what extent do you agree?
3. How does *Ghost Wall* explore the idea of boundaries?
4. *Ghost Wall* is a novel about survival. Discuss.
5. 'Who are the ghosts again, us or our dead?'
   What does *Ghost Wall* suggest about the relationship between the past and the present?
6. *Ghost Wall* suggests that all human beings are capable of cruelty.
   Discuss.
7. *Ghost Wall* shows that the past is ultimately unknowable.
   Do you agree?
8. '... I just think a lot of it's boys playing in the woods.'
   Is this an accurate assessment of the camp?
9. *Ghost Wall* demonstrates the dangers of nostalgia. Discuss.
10. Class differences are the greatest source of tension among the campers in *Ghost Wall*.
    Do you agree?

Vocabulary for writing on *Ghost Wall*

Coercive control: a pattern of controlling and dominating behaviour, usually within the context of a familial relationship.

Liminal: between the threshold of two things or belonging to two states.

Morality: a set of values or beliefs about what constitutes good and bad behaviour.

Nationalism: great love for one's own country, even to the point of regarding it as superior to other countries.

Nostalgia: a fond or sentimental feeling towards the past.

Prehistoric: referring to the time before written historical records.

Prologue: a separate, introductory section of a text, in which background detail or context for the events in the main part of the text is often given.

Xenophobia: prejudice towards any person or thing from another country.

Analysing a sample topic

***Ghost Wall* demonstrates that power always corrupts. Do you agree?**

When analysing an essay topic, it is important to understand precisely what the topic is asking you to do. This means identifying key words and terms, as well as task words such as 'discuss' and 'explore'. In the topic above, the type of question is 'Do you agree?'. This means that you will need to form a contention that expresses your view on the statement in the topic, based on your interpretation of the text.

The key words in the topic are 'power' and 'corrupts'. These words indicate the focus of your response needs to be on power, in any of its forms, and its effects on characters and situations. The modifying word 'always' invites you to challenge the topic statement by considering exceptions. Does the novel include any examples of power being used in a positive way, or characters whose access to power does not negatively impact their moral compass?

Sample introduction

> The main cause of the growing tension among the small group of Iron Age re-enactors in *Ghost Wall* is their differing access to power, whether that be the power to decide what they will eat for breakfast or the power over life and death. Bill and the Professor, the senior men of the group, assume control over proceedings, and their influence, particularly Bill's, slowly impacts the younger men, who in turn begin

to exercise their privilege in subtly malevolent ways. But they are not equally corrupted, suggesting that the corrosive effects of power can be resisted. The novel also suggests that power can be turned to good ends, with both Molly and Trudi using their relative advantages to Silvie's ultimate benefit. Thus *Ghost Wall* suggests that power is not a quality an individual either possesses or doesn't, but must be understood in the context of relationships between individuals or groups. Moreover, the novel implies that men, as a group in relation to women, are generally more susceptible to the lure of power as a means of oppressing or harming others.

Body paragraph outline

Paragraph 1: The men in *Ghost Wall* have the greatest access to power, and each one of them, by the end of the camp, has been corrupted by it.

- Bill is a bully and Professor Slade assumes a natural authority over the others by virtue of his education and status.
- Though Bill and the Professor do not see eye to eye over the purpose and running of the camp, they are united in their passion for history and, it turns out, their propensity for wielding their power violently.
- Dan and Pete begin the novel as apparently rational, reasonable and friendly. But both change during the camp to the point that, by the end, they are willing to exercise their power to collude in Silvie's torture.

Paragraph 2: Though both take part in the ritual re-enactment, Dan displays reservations that Pete does not and ultimately leaves early, suggesting that the corruptive potential of power is not the same for every individual.

- From early on, Pete shows signs of being potentially more susceptible to corruption than Dan; for example, he is less squeamish about the rabbit skinning and chooses to join the men hunting.
- Dan displays a softer, more tender nature than Pete (vomiting at the rabbit skinning, preferring to stay with Silvie and Molly while the other men hunt, offering to joint the rabbits to spare Silvie and Molly); ultimately, his compassion leads him to stop short of harming Silvie at the ceremony.
- Even Bill and the Professor are not wholly corrupt, each displaying some care and tenderness towards Silvie at different points.

Paragraph 3: Some characters, including Molly and Trudi, lack power in some respects – for instance, as women in a patriarchal society – but have power in others, such as their relative privilege, and both choose to use this privilege for the benefit of others.

- Like the male students, Molly could choose to align herself with the more powerful figures in the camp, remaining silent in the face of the injustice she witnesses in order to preserve her own safety and status. Instead she defends both Silvie and Alison, and openly criticises rules and behaviours she disagrees with.
- Trudi, too, has power associated with knowledge and experience, as well as her status within the town. She chooses to use her practical knowledge to treat Silvie's wounds and her familiarity with officialdom to offer assistance in bringing Bill to justice.
- Molly's and Trudi's ability to exercise power in productive rather than oppressive ways seems to be related to their personal qualities and, possibly, their own experiences of being on the disadvantaged side in other relationships with a power imbalance, such as that between men and women.

Sample conclusion

Ghost Wall demonstrates that power has a corruptive tendency but that the effects of this vary widely depending on the personal qualities of the individuals involved and their own experiences of being the victims of oppressive power relations. Bill and the Professor are accustomed to positions of authority and control, and their behaviour at the sacrificial re-enactment suggests that untrammelled power can certainly turn malignant. It also has the potential to erode the moral integrity of some, such as Dan and Pete, though not consistently or to a predictable degree. But others, especially those who have been victims of immoral wielders of power, are capable not only of resisting its corrosive effects but also of using it benevolently, to empower others.

SAMPLE ANSWER

Ghost Wall is a novel about survival. Discuss.

Sarah Moss' novel *Ghost Wall* depicts a summer camp during which the seven participants must live, as far as possible, as Iron Age Britons did, hunting and gathering their own food and without recourse to modern conveniences. But the greatest challenge for protagonist Silvie is not physical survival in the face of deprivation, but emotional and mental survival in the face of her father's ongoing abuse. Her mother, Alison, endures a similar battle. Meanwhile, the Professor and his students must wage a battle for their moral integrity, as the atmosphere at the camp turns darker and tensions mount, until all are tested in a final, dramatic ritual re-enactment that places each of them at risk in different ways.

A primary need for the campers is food, to ensure their physical survival, and the novel is structured around their days spent hunting, foraging and preparing meals from what they can glean from the land. Though Bill and the Professor have some success, for the others the foraging missions are difficult and barely productive. As townswoman Trudi points out, they can't expect the success of their ancestors 'now all the land is farmed', and they are forced to supplement their diet with visits to the Spar convenience store. The attempt to live exactly as Iron Age people did is thus doomed from the beginning, survival being impossible without recourse to modern conveniences.

For Silvie and Alison, though, dominated by the will of an abusive bully, a more difficult and complex challenge than subsistence is the fight to survive with not only their physical but also their mental and emotional health intact. In order to do this, they adopt a variety of strategies, chiefly appeasement of the aggressive Bill. Alison accepts the abuse as her due – 'it were my fault' she tells Silvie when Bill leaves bruises on her arm for letting the fire go out. Silvie, too, is mostly obedient towards her father but is unable to entirely control her streak of independence – 'you court it' her mother tells her when Bill slaps her for cheekiness. There is evidence that others outside the family are aware of Bill's violence. Silvie recalls the mother of a schoolfriend, Claire, telling her about her sister who fled an abusive marriage, in such a way as to suggest she is hoping to broach the tricky subject with Silvie, with the aim of getting her to open up. But Silvie receives this information blandly and quickly changes the subject, far too afraid of her father's wrath to risk confiding in anyone outside the family – another survival strategy that keeps her father's rage at least somewhat contained.

Bill's violence might be understood as his own maladaptive and unreasonable survival strategy, allowing him to cope with the inferiority he feels at not having achieved the success of 'those other men who were paid to walk the places [he] loved and write the ideas he could have had'. Bullying his family allows him to feel some semblance of control over the life 'he weren't meant for', dreaming as he does of a nobler existence, with 'his own ancestry ... a lineage, a claim on something'. Set in his ways and convinced of his rightness, Bill changes little over the course of the camp, only becoming more willing to exercise ultimate control over the daughter the Professor reminds him is 'your sacrifice'. Ultimately, Bill's coerciveness is demonstrated to be an ineffective survival strategy, as the power of the law proves stronger than his own power.

In contrast, the male students are significantly transformed by their camping experience, unwittingly placed in a position where the survival of their moral integrity is at stake. The heavy shadow of the past over their endeavour, together with Bill's simmering anger and resentment, has a corrosive effect on the young men, encouraging them to behave in ways they presumably would not have dreamed of prior to the camp. Pete, having previously 'nearly vommed' at the skinning of the rabbits, elects to hunt with Bill and the Professor. Dan, who had mocked the rabbit skulls, 'with their little teeth', that made up the ghost wall, ends by working 'seriously' on the wall's construction. Both boys are also, at least initially, willing to take part in the sacrifice re-enactment – although

Dan ultimately does not go through with this – indicating that their moral boundaries have in fact not survived the camping experience but have, to varying degrees, been eroded by the poisonous atmosphere and the example of the older men.

The ritual is also the culmination of Silvie's struggle for both her physical health – indeed, her very life – and her spiritual survival, as she faces a future hopefully free from abuse and yet inevitably shadowed by its legacy. From the beginning of the camp she has been wondering, 'how do you leave home, how do you get away, how do you not go back?' knowing that escape is necessary for her survival but unable to imagine it being truly possible. It takes being brought to the brink of death by her father's monstrous possessiveness, because she 'was the scapegoat, the sacrifice, the thing Dad wanted to keep', and her subsequent rescue by Molly, for this path to freedom to open to her. When Bill is arrested by the police, he loses his battle for control not only over his family but over all the campers. Silvie and, hopefully, Alison are finally freed. Silvie has survived not only the physical attack during the ritual re-enactment, but years of physical and mental abuse at the hands of her father; the novel's closing image of Molly and Silvie entwined on the bed at Trudi's house sounds a cautiously optimistic note that celebrates the human capacity for endurance.

REFERENCES

Text

Moss, S 2018, *Ghost Wall*, Granta, London.

References and further reading

Brockes, E 2021, 'Sarah Moss: The rhetoric during lockdown was terrifying', *The Guardian*, 29 October, https://www.theguardian.com/books/2021/oct/29/sarah-moss-the-rhetoric-during-lockdown-was-terrifying

Clark, A 2021, 'Novelist Sarah Moss: "The injustice of the lockdown made my blood boil"', *The Irish Times*, 10 November, https://www.irishtimes.com/culture/books/novelist-sarah-moss-the-injustice-of-the-lockdown-made-my-blood-boil-1.4722645

Crown, S 2018, '*Ghost Wall* by Sarah Moss review – back to the iron age', *The Guardian*, 28 September, https://www.theguardian.com/books/2018/sep/28/ghost-wall-sarah-moss-review

Hagy, A 2019, 'Characters who crave a return to the past, human sacrifice and all', *The New York Times*, 11 January, https://www.nytimes.com/2019/01/11/books/review/sarah-moss-ghost-wall.html

Hansen, D 2019, 'The slippery "ghost wall" warns against the dangers of nativism and nostalgia', *Chicago Review of Books*, 22 February, https://chireviewofbooks.com/2019/02/22/the-slippery-ghost-wall-warns-against-the-dangers-of-nativism-and-nostalgia/

Hilts, C 2021, 'Touching the past: encountering Iron Age bog bodies', *Current Archaeology*, no. 375, 1 May, https://the-past.com/feature/touching-the-past-encountering-iron-age-bog-bodies/

Hyde, J 2018, '*Ghost Wall* review: Sarah Moss' novel about power, consent and domestic violence', *The Sydney Morning Herald*, 20 December, https://www.smh.com.au/entertainment/books/ghost-wall-review-sarah-moss-novel-about-power-consent-and-domestic-violence-20181219-h19aoi.html

Moss, S 2020, 'Love thy neighbour? Sarah Moss on the darker side of community in a crisis', *The Guardian*, 22 August, https://www.theguardian.com/books/2020/aug/22/love-thy-neighbour-sarah-moss-on-the-darker-side-of-community-in-a-crisis

Moss, S 2022, 'A moment that changed me: I was crippled by negative thoughts – then I bought a silver bracelet', *The Guardian*, 12 January, https://www.theguardian.com/lifeandstyle/2022/jan/12/a-moment-that-changed-me-i-was-crippled-by-negative-thoughts-then-i-bought-a-silver-bracelet

Quinn, A 2019, '*Ghost Wall* explores the human cost of nativist nostalgia', *The Atlantic*, 25 January, https://www.theatlantic.com/entertainment/archive/2019/01/ghost-wall-more-brexit-parable-review/581068/

Russell, M 2020, 'The Celts in Britain: everything you need to know', *History Extra*, 18 August, https://www.historyextra.com/period/iron-age/celts-britain-romans-who-were-they-human-sacrifice/

Talbot, M 2019, 'Sarah Moss's "Ghost Wall," a slender novel that evokes existential dread', *The New Yorker*, 2 January, https://www.newyorker.com/recommends/read/sarah-mosss-ghost-wall-a-slender-novel-that-evokes-existential-dread

Women's Prize Trust n.d., 'Archives: A Q&A with Sarah Moss', Women's Prize Trust, https://womensprize.com/archives-a-qa-with-sarah-moss/